G000242305

Embroidered
Projects

H. Faqeant

Embroidered Projects

Sue Hawkins

David & Charles

Dedication

For Cherry

A DAVID & CHARLES BOOK

First published in the UK in 2003

Copyright © Sue Hawkins 2003

Distributed in North America
by F&W Publications, Inc.
4700 East Galbraith Road
Cincinnati, OH 45236
1-800-289-0963

Sue Hawkins has asserted her right to be identified as author of this work
in accordance with the Copyright, Designs and Patents Act, 1988.

All rights reserved. No part of this publication may be reproduced, stored
in a retrieval system, or transmitted, in any form or by any means,
electronic or mechanical, by photocopying, recording or otherwise,
without prior permission in writing from the publisher.

The designs in this book are copyright and must not be made for resale.
However, they may be copied and made for personal use.

A catalogue record for this book is available from the British Library.

ISBN 0 7153 1433 5 paperback

Printed in China by Leefung-Asco
For David & Charles
Brunel House   Newton Abbot   Devon

Executive Editor   Cheryl Brown
Desk Editor   Jennifer Proverbs
Executive Art Editor   Ali Myer
Senior Designer   Prudence Rogers
Copy-editor   Linda Clements
Production Controller   Ros Napper

Visit our website at www.davidandcharles.co.uk

David & Charles books are available from all good bookshops;
alternatively you can contact our Orderline on (0)1626 334555
or write to us at FREEPOST EX2110, David & Charles *Direct*,
Newton Abbot TQ12 4ZZ (No stamp required UK mainland).

DOLLS HOUSE DO-IT-YOURSELF

Embroidered Projects

Contents

Introduction

This is a selection of soft furnishings for the dolls' house in a variety of styles all for the $\frac{1}{12}$ scale model maker. They are all the decorative touches that make a house a home and have to be carefully made rather than bought – there is a certain charm that cannot be purchased at any price. I have included designs suitable for many historical periods and styles of decoration including Regency, Edwardian, Georgian, Victorian, Art Deco and Art Nouveau. Some of the projects are designed to co-ordinate with the projects in my first book in this series, *Carpets and Rugs*.

Most of the projects are worked from a coloured chart with symbols added where shades of a colour are close to help you distinguish the difference. Designs that are not charted can be traced from a simple line drawing and then embroidered using free embroidery stitches. All the stitches used are explained on pages 11–13. I have worked in a variety of threads, including wool, cotton (floss) and silk. Many of the projects are so small that they only use a tiny amount of any one colour – you may find this useful as you can substitute from your own collection of threads rather than rushing out to buy new. I would, however, advise sticking to natural fibres rather than anything man-made. Experiment with colour schemes to suit you and match the décor that you already have in your dolls' house.

Detailed instructions for the actual embroideries are given under the project headings: for more general instructions turn to the section on making up starting on page 15. Some of the pieces of furniture were already finished and upholstered when I bought them and some were available in kit form

and designed specifically to take embroidery. I tried to use pieces that are easily available so they can be repeated – see the list in Suppliers on page 62. If you already have furniture you want to cover you should find the designs easy to adapt to different shapes by simply adding or subtracting background.

I would like to think this selection of projects will set you going and be the inspiration for you to make some of these and then branch out into your own designs as your ideas grow out of mine. The finer the canvas that you are able to work the more authentic your miniature will look but do not torture yourself or your eyes. Having said that, I did notice as I worked my way through that what seemed very fine when I started became quite normal as my eyes became used to the fine gauze. But embroidery should

always be a pleasure and it will always show if joy was lacking in the making, so resort to a slightly lesser count of fabric if you need to and enjoy your stitching.

Lastly, I make no apologies for how delicate and fine these projects are – they have to be to be the correct scale but then I am assuming that if you didn't relish attention to detail you wouldn't have a dolls' house in the first place!

Materials and Equipment

This section contains helpful, illustrated information on the basic materials and equipment you will need to stitch the projects as shown in this book, including useful tools to make working easier and also the embroidery fabrics and threads you can use to achieve the most attractive and realistic results.

Embroidery Fabrics

Silk gauze Silk can be spun into a very fine thread that is still strong enough to make a very fine canvas and it is available in very high counts. The projects that are worked on gauze in this book are all worked on either 32 or 40 count. It is expensive so be careful how you cut the pieces for working. In order that you do not waste too much it is a good idea to mount the gauze into a piece of calico or curtain lining before you stretch it in an embroidery frame or hoop (see page 10). Alternatively some shops sell silk gauze already mounted in card mounts.

Canvas The Victorian cushion and seat cover on page 32 are worked on 20 count double canvas (previously called Penelope canvas). The canvas threads are grouped in pairs and double threads can be worked over to make larger stitches. It is also possible to split the double threads to make a single canvas that is twice the count to work some of the design as petit point. This technique was commonly used in Victorian embroidery, with flowers or faces for example, where more detail was required. To split the threads use a size 24 tapestry needle and prick the closer intersections to spread them. The seat squab on page 44 is worked on 22 count mono canvas.

Linen Linen is an evenweave fabric normally used for cross stitch but it is also ideal for miniature embroidery projects featuring other stitches, such as the blackwork table cover on page 28. Blackwork is a counted thread technique, in this case worked on fine 36 count linen.

Surface embroidery fabrics A fine, closely woven fabric is needed for the surface embroidery projects. Ordinary cotton sateen-finish curtain lining or cotton chintz are ideal for the folding screen on page 39 and the fire screen on page 42. A softer fabric will be needed for the bed linen on page 56 – very fine cotton lawn or soft handkerchief linen are both ideal.

General Equipment

If you are already interested in needlework you will undoubtedly have a collection of tools and accessories, some essential and some old favourites! The basics you will need are described here.

Scissors A pair of sharp scissors for cutting fabric will be needed, plus a small sharp pair of embroidery scissors for threads. You will also need an unpicker in the event of stitching mistakes.

Embroidery frames It is better to use a frame when stitching small projects to keep work stable. There are many types of frame available so choose one that you are most comfortable with. Follow the manufacturer's instructions for mounting the fabric. See page 10 for stitching silk gauze into a fabric mount. Never put your embroidery between the rings of an embroidery hoop – it will squash it at best and damage it at worst.

Magnifiers Do not struggle with your eyesight; buy a magnifier if you have difficulty. There are many different types available: some sit on your chest, some clip on to your glasses and some are fixed to a stand with integral lighting. Find the one that suits you best, perhaps taking some embroidery to the shop to try it before you purchase. Daylight simulation bulbs are also helpful, especially when stitching with pastel shades at night.

Thread organizers There are various systems to organize and hold threads that you are working with. Manufacturers' colour charts are invaluable if you are planning to design for yourself or change some of the colours used in the projects – ask at your local needlework shop.

Masking tape This is useful for edging canvas to prevent snagging but do not buy the three-day variety – it is designed not to stick too well!

Fray Check This is a transparent fabric glue to seal fabric edges and prevent fraying Do not worry if it seems to darken colours when you apply it as it becomes transparent as it dries. If you are in any doubt try it on spare thread before you use it on your precious stitching.

Fabric markers There are different types of markers in the shops but most are not fine enough for these tiny designs. An H pencil with a very sharp point is best, but make sure that the line you draw is fine enough to be completely covered by your stitching. If you do make a mistake a soft rubber eraser works on fabric, though not as well as on paper, and should improve the situation.

Needles

Tapestry needles It is best to use these when working on silk gauze or canvas as they are blunt and pass through without catching. The size required will vary according to the number of strands and the gauge of canvas being used but for all these projects a 26 or even a finer 28 will be suitable. As you stitch, move the needle along the thread to stop it wearing in one place. Drop the needle every now and then and let it hang freely to allow the thread to untwist. Do treat yourself to a gold-plated needle for this fine work: it will never tarnish and remain beautifully smooth and a pleasure to use.

Sharp needles For the projects that are worked in surface embroidery use a fine needle with a sharp point, a size 10 Straw is ideal.

Threads

There is a wide variety of yarns and threads on the market and stitchers seem to have their own particular favourites. The projects in this book use various threads to create different effects and these are described below. The projects are all so small that some of them use only tiny amounts of a colour, so do substitute from your own collection for economy.

DMC stranded cotton This six-stranded mercerized embroidery cotton (floss) is readily available and a single strand is fine enough for use on 40 count silk gauze. Two strands cover 32 count perfectly and have been used for the majority of projects in this book. DMC stranded cottons were used but if you prefer to stitch with Anchor threads, the conversions are supplied within the projects.

DMC Medici wool This is a very fine embroidery wool (yarn) that is ideal for miniature work. It is used in the Victorian projects that have the design worked in stranded cotton but backgrounds in wool to give a matt effect behind the shinier design.

Appletons crewel wool This range of fine wools (yarns) is easy to use, fine enough for the finest canvas and available in a large range of colours with each colour produced in a carefully graded range of shades.

Danish Flower threads These attractive threads are made from single-ply cotton (floss) and have been used for the William Morris Cushion. They are perfect when you wish to produce a matt finish.

Caron Soie Cristale This is a pure silk twelve-stranded thread with a beautiful lustre. It has been used to simulate shiny brocade on the Georgian seat cover and also for the Regency fire screen because it is so pliable for fine surface embroidery.

Basic Techniques

The following information will help you produce perfect results, describing how to use the charts, calculate design sizes so that you can adapt the charts for your own use, begin work neatly and work all the stitches featured in the book.

Using the Charts

Most of the projects are stitched from colour charts and where there are close colours symbols have been added to distinguish different shades. One square on the chart represents one stitch on the canvas. Arrows at the sides of the charts make finding the centre easy — it is generally best to start there to avoid working off centre or even off the edge of the canvas. Work the design first, stitching in areas of colour and then fill in backgrounds.

Calculating Finished Sizes

Finished sizes are given for all the designs in this book but if you want to change the gauze or canvas mesh size it will alter the size of your finished piece. To calculate the finished size of any design you need to know the stitch counts, that is the total number of chart squares across a design, both ways. Divide these counts by the count per inch of the gauze or canvas you want to use and this will give you the dimensions of the finished piece. Two examples are given below.

How to calculate finished sizes

Example:
If the stitch count is 64 x 48 on
an 32 count gauze;
64 ÷ 32 = 2
48 ÷ 32 = 1.5
Therefore the finished size is 2in x 1½in
(To change to metric, multiply by 2.5
i.e. 5 x 3.8cm)

Example:
If the stitch count is 64 x 48 on
a 40 count silk gauze;
64 ÷ 40 = 1.6
48 ÷ 40 = 1.2
Therefore the finished size is 1.6in x 1.2in
(1⁹⁄₁₆ x 1³⁄₁₆in)
(To change to metric, multiply by 2.5
i.e. 4 x 3cm)

How Many Strands?

Throughout the projects, the number of strands of thread needed is given. The number you use will vary according to the thickness of the thread, the size of the gauze or canvas and the effect you want to achieve. Too few strands and the base fabric will show through; too many strands and it will be difficult to pull the thread through the fabric and result in thick, clumsy-looking work. If in doubt, try a little on a spare piece of fabric. If you are using more than one strand of stranded cotton (floss) always pull the strands apart and then recombine them to stitch as this removes the twist and will make your stitching smoother.

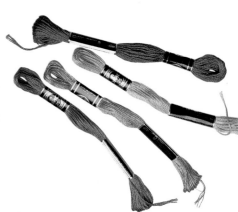

Stitching Gauze into a Fabric Mount

For the most economic use of silk gauze and for ease of working, it is advisable to stitch the gauze into a fabric mount. Cut a piece of calico to fit your frame and then cut a window in the middle, a little bigger than the project. Overlock (oversew) the edges of the fabric and the window to prevent fraying. Now cut a piece of silk gauze a little large than the window. Fold it in four to find the centre and mark the centre point with a thread – this can be removed as soon as the first few stitches are in place. It is a good idea to knot the ends of this thread together so it does not fall out until you are ready to remove it. Now sew it into the window either with a sewing machine on a long stitch or by hand. Once the project is finished you can unpick the sewing and re-use the mount over and over again.

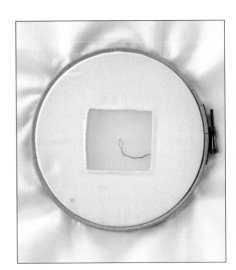

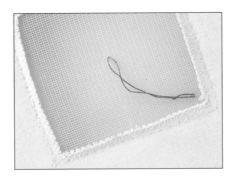

Starting and Finishing Stitching

To produce the best results it is advisable to start and finish your stitching neatly. There are two methods of starting: a looped start and a waste knot start. A looped start can only be used with an even number of threads, whereas a waste knot start can use any number of threads.

To begin with a looped start with two strands, take a single thread that is twice the length that you need, fold it in half and thread the two ends through the needle leaving the loop at the other end. Push the needle up through the fabric with your first stitch and down again, leaving the loop hanging at the back of the canvas. Now pass the needle through the loop and pull, thus anchoring the thread.

To begin with a waste knot start by knotting the end of the thread and pulling it through your canvas about 1in (2.5cm) from where you intend to begin stitching, leaving the knot on the top. Work your stitches towards the knot, catching the starting thread into the back of the stitches. When you reach the knot cut it off.

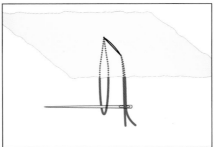

Loop start

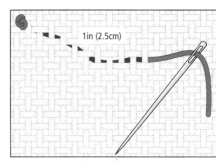

Waste knot start

To finish off your stitching neatly, run the thread under a few stitches on the back and snip off the thread. Do this carefully so that you do not alter the tension of the existing stitches on the front of the canvas. To begin a new length of thread or a new colour, run the thread under a few stitches on the back before you begin to stitch. Do not run a dark colour through lighter stitches as it may show through on the front.

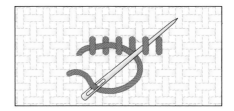

Finishing off neatly

Working the Stitches

The stitches used in the book are all simple to work. Some are commonly used for counted thread work while others are used in surface embroidery.

Back Stitch

Back stitch is used for the blackwork table cover. Take care not to pass the dark-coloured thread over the back of the work as it will show through on the front. Following the diagram, bring the needle up at 1, down at 2, up at 3, down at 4 and so on.

Chain Stitch

This is a surface embroidery stitch which is used most effectively in the Art Nouveau folding screen. Follow the diagrams, bringing the needle up through the fabric to start at 1. Go down at 2, forming a loop of thread as you do so and bring the needle up in the loop at 3. Pull the thread gently to make the first loop of the chain. Repeat to work the whole chain. Do not pull the thread too tightly, allowing the loops to remain rounded. To finish the chain, catch down the last loop with a small stitch.

Detached Chain Stitch

This simple little stitch is used on the Edwardian bed linen to create individual petals. Follow the diagrams, bringing the needle up through the fabric at 1, then down at 2, forming a loop in the thread. Hold the loop and make a small stitch to catch the loop down by bringing the needle up at 3 through the loop, then down at 4.

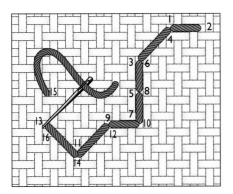

Back stitch

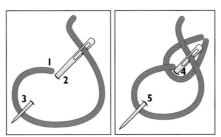

Chain stitch

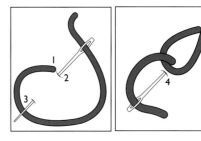

Detached chain stitch

11

Cross Stitch

This is a very commonly used stitch in embroidery and has been used on double canvas as the backgrounds to the Victorian cushion and chair cover. Follow the number sequence in the diagram, starting at the bottom left corner and crossing diagonally to top right. Bring the needle back up at the bottom right corner and cross to the top left corner to complete the stitch. For neater stitching, work all the cross stitches with the top diagonally in the same direction.

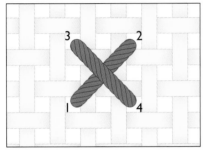

Cross stitch

Long and Short Stitch

This stitch has been used in the Regency fire screen. Only the first row worked has long and short stitches, the following rows are all long (see diagrams). Begin at the outside edge and then stitch the following rows into the stitches already worked, splitting the threads to blend the stitches and colours. Don't be afraid to make the stitches longer than you feel you should as they will be shortened by the next layer of stitching. Don't try to follow the diagrams too rigidly – use them as a guide and adapt them to the shape that you have to fill.

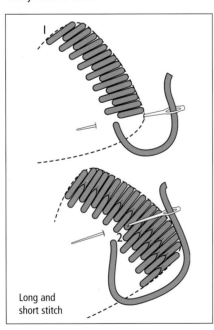

Long and short stitch

French Knots

These little stitches are used to add detail and texture. Following the diagram, bring your needle up through the fabric, hold the thread taut and wind the needle once around the thread. Pull the twist down on to the surface of the fabric and insert the needle into almost the same place as it came out (but not quite or your knot will disappear through the hole). Pull the needle carefully through the fabric still keeping tension on the thread until you have to let go. French knots are usually created with thread wound twice around the needle but these are shown wound only once to make them smaller.

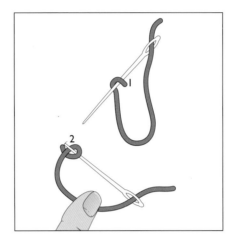

French knot

Long-legged Cross Stitch

This stitch produces a braided effect that is very useful for edging. When worked in the hand and pulled quite tightly it naturally turns over the edge and so is very useful for edging tiny cushions. Simply follow the number sequence in the diagrams.

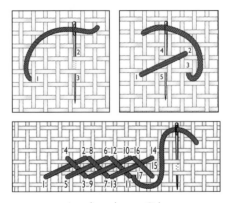

Long-legged cross stitch

Herringbone Stitch

This versatile stitch has been used to hold back the edges of fabric. Follow the diagrams to work the stitch and when making the upper part of the stitch, work through the turned-over edge and into the back of the embroidery to make it firmer.

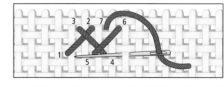

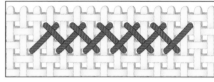

Herringbone stitch

Satin Stitch

This is simply straight, flat stitches laid side by side, the length of the stitches varied to fill the shape of the petal or leaf. In order that your stitches lie closely and neatly beside each other always come up the same side and down on the other so that you cover the back of the fabric as well. To work a leaf with a central vein work the stitches more closely together in the centre than at the tip so they radiate as they work around the end of the leaf, i.e., true satin stitch on each side with straight stitches at the tip.

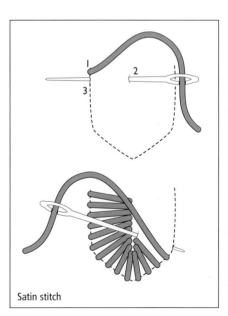

Satin stitch

Simple Hem Stitch

This is a method of sealing the edge of linen in the simplest way and is used on the edge of the blackwork table cover. Work the stitches fairly tightly so that when you cut away the edge you do not cut any loose threads. Following the diagrams, work a straight stitch across two threads, turning the needle to face horizontally. Make another straight stitch across two threads at right angles to the first stitch, then pass the needle down diagonally under two threads. Repeat the straight stitches along the row, counting carefully. After the hem stitching is complete the fabric may be cut away.

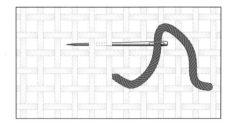

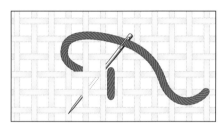

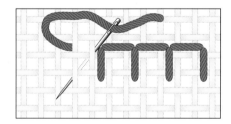

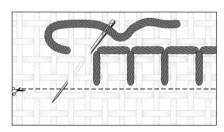

Simple hem stitch

Tent Stitch

Most of the projects are worked using tent stitch. There are two methods of working this stitch: diagonal and continental (see diagrams). Diagonal tent stitch distorts the canvas less, especially when you are working backgrounds and in rows. Continental tent stitch is easier to work when stitching individual motifs and irregular-shaped parts of a design.

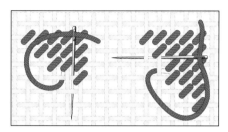

Diagonal tent stitch

Continental tent stitch

Stem Stitch

This useful stitch is used to create lines and curves. Follow the diagrams, holding the thread down with your finger each time you make a stitch to keep it out of the way and also to maintain an even tension. Try to make your stitches equal in length all along the line but if there is a tight curve to get round it will help to shorten the stitches a little.

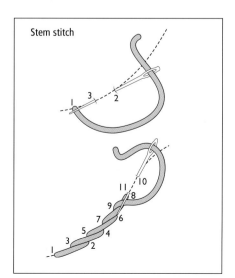

Stem stitch

The Georgian seat cover uses both diagonal and continental tent stitch.

Split Back Stitch

This stitch has been used in the Regency fire screen and is similar to ordinary back stitch except that the needle is inserted into the previous stitch. Take care to actually split the thread with your needle. You will find that you can make very smooth curves by making each stitch curve a little as you split it.

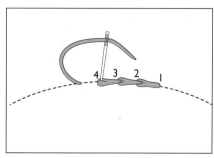

Split back stitch

13

Making Up the Projects

This section gives advice on how to finish your miniature projects beautifully – how to frame embroidery in pictures, make your work up as cushions, seat covers and bell pulls, and how to add finishing touches such as cords and tassels.

Pressing Your Work

These instructions apply to all the projects. Even though you have worked on a frame your embroidery will be a little distorted so you need to pull it gently back into shape.

Place a layer of towel on your ironing board and lay the embroidery face down on the towelling. With your iron on the steam setting hold it over the embroidery allowing the steam to blow over the back of your work but do not press it down. Pick up the work, which will be softened by the steam, and pull it back to square. Now lay it back down and press it to fix the shape. Allow it to get cold before you pick it up so it does not go out of shape again. Never press on the right side as you will flatten the stitches and take the sheen off the thread.

Framing Samplers and Pictures

To mount samplers and pictures you will need some backing card, fabric glue and a picture frame (see Suppliers page 62). The alphabet sampler is mounted on grey card and the other two samplers and the William Morris picture are on cream. Because the colour of the card shows through the silk gauze it is important to choose a colour that makes the embroidery show up.

1 Cut a piece of card to the size of the frame aperture. Cover it with a thin layer of fabric glue and allow it to become tacky.

2 Smooth the embroidery squarely on to the glued card and allow it to dry. Trim the fabric to the same size as the card.

3 Place the mounted embroidery in the frame. Glue on the frame backing, or cut another piece of card if the frame did not have a back.

Framed alphabet sampler

Making Twisted Cord

Twisted cords are useful for trimming chair seats, for edging cushions and for hanging bell pulls.

1 Take lengths of stranded cotton (floss) in colours to match your project. Twist the lengths tightly and then fold it in half without letting go of the ends – the lengths will twist up on themselves to make a cord.

2 Tie a knot at each end to prevent the cord from untwisting.

Edging on the Mackintosh chair cover

Hanging loop on Victorian bell pull

Making Tiny Tassels

These trimmings make attractive decorations on the corners of cushions, as in the Tudor Rose floor cushion and the Chinoiserie bolster.

1 Take sixteen strands of stranded cotton (floss) each about 2in (5cm) long and arrange them in a pile with all the ends together.

2 Take another two strands about 8in (20cm) long, double one and twist it tightly. Loop it around the mid point of the tassel strands so that the tassel lies in the loop and then allow it to twist to make a cord for the tassel. Knot the ends together.

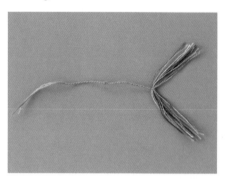

3 Thread both ends of the other 8in (20cm) length in your needle so you have a loop at the bottom. Fold the tassel at the cord and lay the loop around just below the fold. Pass the needle through the loop and pull up tightly. Wind around again and finish off securely by stitching through the windings, leaving the ends hanging amongst the tassel threads. Now cut the tassel off to the required length.

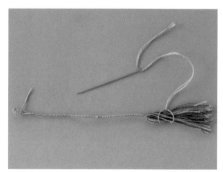

Making a Plain Cushion

The cushions in the book have a long-legged cross-stitched edge to create a braided effect and are backed with silk dupion (see Suppliers page 62) or cotton chintz in a colour that picks out one of the colours in the design. They are all filled with natural kapok which is very soft and fine, although you could use polyester instead. The little cushions are too small to make the way you would a full-size one (by making it inside out and turning to the right side). It is too difficult to turn something this size right side out and also crumples your lovely, flat embroidery, therefore it is much better to do all the stitching from the outside.

1 Trim the silk gauze or canvas to ⅜in (1cm) of the edge of the embroidery and then cut a piece of backing fabric the same size.

2 Fold in the edge of the gauze or canvas; an edging of long-legged cross stitch makes it fold well and sit like a braid on the edge. Fold the edges of the backing fabric into the same size and slipstitch the backing to the cushion front. Begin stitching on one side a little way from a corner, stitch around this corner and around three sides until you reach the other end of the first side.

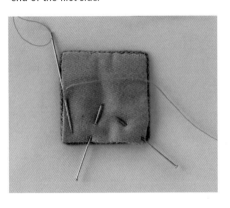

3 Put the needle aside and fill the cushion with polyester stuffing via the gap and then slipstitch the opening closed.

Making a Tasselled Cushion

Adding tassels to a cushion is an attractive finishing touch. The Victorian cushion, Tudor rose cushion and Chinoiserie bolster all feature them.

1 Make four tassels (see previous page) from the embroidery threads used for the cushion front. Knot the cords close to the top of the tassels to make short stalks on each one.

2 Make the cushion in the same way as a plain one as described above but tuck a tassel into the seam at each corner as you stitch, making sure that the knot on the cord is inside the seam to prevent the tassel being pulled off.

Tasselled bolster cushion

Victorian cushion with matching tassels

Fitting a Seat Cover

The Victorian chair and Mackintosh chair were supplied with covers so these need to be removed. They are glued on but can be prised off carefully and the foam pad reused once the cover is removed. You can add a trimming to your chair to conceal the edge of the embroidery. The Mackintosh chair is trimmed with a length of twisted cord and the Victorian chair with a piece of ready-made braid (see picture below and Suppliers page 62). The Georgian chair was intended for embroidery and came with a loose pad that fitted into a recess in the wood so no trimming was necessary but the pad was covered as in step 1 below.

1 Put some double-sided adhesive tape on the underside of the foam pad. Trim the silk gauze or canvas to ½in (1.25cm) of the embroidery edge and stretch the embroidery over the top of the foam pad. Fold the edges over to the back and secure on the double-sided tape.

2 Take the piece of trimming and pin it around the embroidery on the pad on the front and sides and then cut each end to allow ½in (1.25cm) to tuck in under the pad. Using clear multi-purpose adhesive, glue the ends in under the pad and once the glue has dried remove the pins so that you have a loop that fits the front and sides but is not yet attached.

3 Glue the seat pad to the seat and hold it down firmly until the glue is dry (clothes pegs are useful for this). Finally, glue the loop of trimming over the edge of the embroidery.

Victorian seat cover with a braid edging

The
Projects

Victorian Samplers

Full-size samplers such as these would be worked in cross stitch but at this scale cross stitch is too bulky so these have been worked in tent stitch in order to make them very small. They use just one strand of stranded cotton (floss) on 40 count silk gauze. You need to be very careful not to run any threads across the back of your work because they will show through the gauze where it is not covered with stitching.

In the 18th century samplers were the means by which young girls learnt their needlecraft skills. Some, like this little band sampler (far right), were used as a record of different stitches and for practice. Band samplers were sometimes worked on a long strip of fabric and kept rolled up and used simply as a reference; others were worked in bands next to each other on a rectangle of fabric.

Poor children in schools and orphanages were taught more basic skills and alphabets were very popular because they taught the children their letters, a skill needed if they were taken into service, to mark household linen. Alphabet samplers were often monochrome and mostly in red. This alphabet is a copy of an 18th century one that has the J missing and slightly irregular lettering.

You will need

2½ x 2½in (6 x 6cm)
40 count silk gauze

Size 28 tapestry needle

Stranded cotton (floss) as follows:
DMC dark red 347 (Anchor 47)

Alphabet Sampler

1 Fold the silk gauze in four to find the centre, mark it with a loose thread and stitch the gauze into a fabric mount (see page 10). This sampler is much easier to work from the top left corner so, having found the centre, you can find the top left corner by measuring ½in (1.25cm) left and ½in (1.25cm) up.

2 Using one strand of stranded cotton (floss), work the design over one fabric thread from the chart on page 18, using continental tent stitch (see page 13). Begin with the border and then work the letters row by row, from the top to the bottom.

3 Remove the finished sampler from the fabric mount and refer to page 14 for pressing and framing.

17

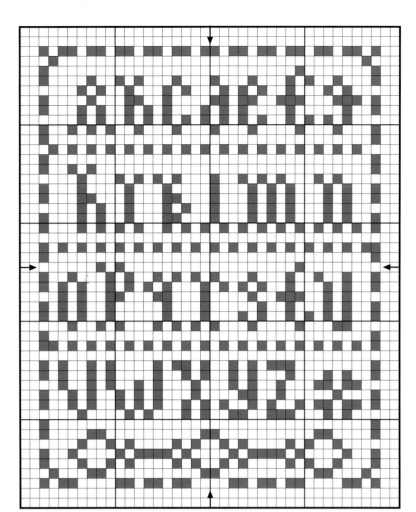

Alphabet Sampler

	DMC	Anchor
■	**347**	**47**

Stitch count 36 x 45
Finished size ¹⁵⁄₁₆ x 1⅛in (2.3 x 2.9cm)
Shown larger than actual size

Band Sampler

You will need

2½ x 2½in (6 x 6cm) 40 count silk gauze

Size 28 tapestry needle

**DMC stranded cotton (floss) as follows
(Anchor conversions in brackets):**

dark pink 3721 (896)

light pink 3712 (895)

dark green 732 (281)

light green 734 (282)

mauve 3041 (872)

blue 931 (977)

yellow 725 (305)

1 Fold the silk gauze in four to find the centre, mark it with a loose thread and stitch the gauze into a fabric mount (see page 10). A sampler such as this is much easier to work from the top left corner so having found the centre by folding you can easily find the top left corner by measuring ½in (1.25cm) left and ½in (1.25cm) up.

2 Using one strand of stranded cotton (floss) throughout, work the design over one fabric thread from the chart, right, using continental tent stitch (see page 13). Work the left-hand rows first and then the broken line down the centre followed by the right-hand rows.

3 Remove the finished sampler from the fabric mount and refer to page 14 for pressing and framing.

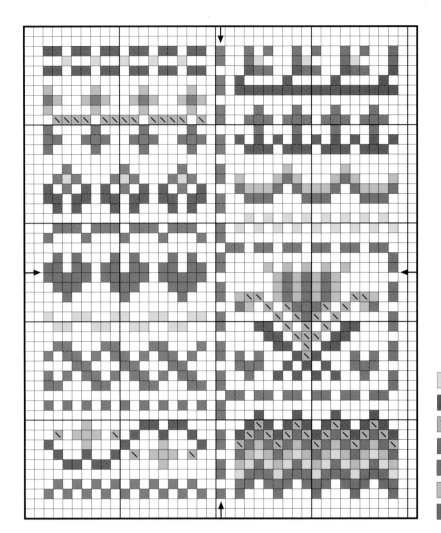

Band Sampler

DMC	Anchor
725	305
732	281
734	282
931	977
3041	872
3712	895
3721	896

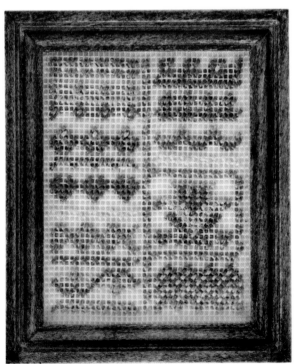

Stitch count 37 x 46
Finished size ¹⁵⁄₁₆ x 1⅛in (2.3 x 2.9cm)
Shown larger than actual size

Georgian Seat Cover and Cushion

These typically Georgian designs can easily be adapted to suit different colour schemes. The cushion has only three shades of gold which could be changed to three shades of another colour – try soft corals and greens for a gentler décor.

Regency stripes were usually found on shiny brocaded fabrics, so the chair seat is worked in pure silk threads to add extra sheen to the stitches. The deep red could be changed to blue or green and the little sprigs on the stripes will still be fine. Check the measurements of your chair and alter the size of the piece to suit; it will be easy to work a little more of the simple repeating pattern. Alternatively, you could square off the sides to make a cushion in blue and gold stripes to match the Greek-styled one.

The flowing design of the central area of the cushion contrasting with the formal border is typical of the Georgian period. Many influences came from travels abroad which were fashionable for the wealthy classes, and this cushion design would have originated in Greece.

Most people have heard of Regency stripes and the seat cover design has a little sprigged motif added. In England, Regency style was named after the Prince Regent who later became George IV. So while the Georgian period covers the years between 1714 and 1810, the Regency period sits within it, beginning about 1790. At this point in time textiles became much more affordable and fashion became something that the middle classes could aspire to as well as the nobility.

Georgian Seat Cover

You will need

3 x 3in (7.5 x 7.5cm) 32 count silk gauze

Size 28 tapestry needle

Caron Soie Cristale silk thread as follows:
purple 6021; red 2013;
pink 2032; cream 4007;
yellow 4003; green 5002

1 Fold the silk gauze in four to find the centre, mark it with a loose thread and stitch the gauze into a fabric mount (see page 10).

2 Using two strands of Caron Soie Cristale, work the design over one fabric thread from the chart, right, using continental tent stitch (see page 13) for the design and then diagonal tent stitch for the wide stripes.

3 Remove the embroidery from the fabric mount and press carefully on the back (see page 14).

4 Cover the seat pad and fix it to your chair (see page 15 for instructions and page 62 for chair suppliers).

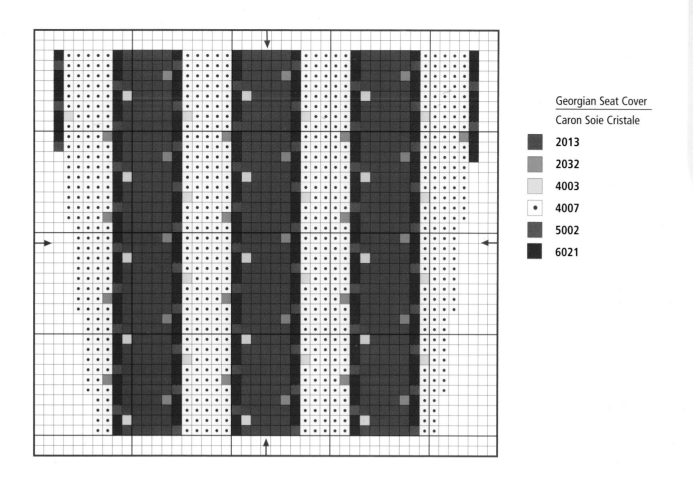

Georgian Seat Cover
Caron Soie Cristale

■	2013
■	2032
□	4003
·	4007
■	5002
■	6021

Stitch count 43 x 38
Finished size 1⅜ x 1³⁄₁₆in (3.4 x 3cm)
Shown larger than actual size

Georgian Cushion

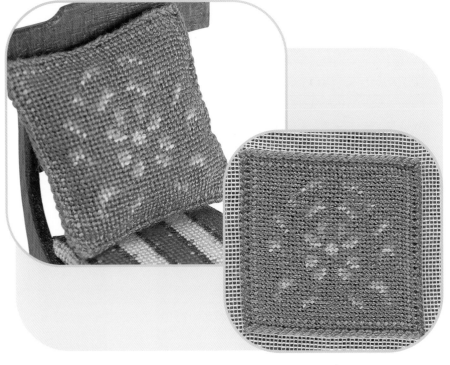

You will need

3 x 3in (7.5 x 7.5cm) 32 count silk gauze

Size 28 tapestry needle

DMC stranded cotton (floss) as follows
(Anchor conversions in brackets):

dark gold 781 (309)

mid gold 783 (307)

light gold 676 (301)

blue 931 (977)

1 Fold the silk gauze in four to find the centre, mark it with a loose thread and stitch the gauze into a fabric mount (see page 10).

2 Using two strands of stranded cotton (floss), work the design over one fabric thread from the chart, using continental tent stitch (see page 13) for the design and then diagonal tent stitch for the background.

3 Remove the embroidery from the fabric mount and press it carefully on the back (see page 14). Using two strands of dark gold, work a row of long-legged cross stitch (see page 12) around the edge of the square. Work in your hand and pull the stitches quite tightly and you will find that this stitch naturally folds the edge of the gauze and so makes a braided edge to your cushion. Refer to page 15 for making up the cushion.

Stitch count 41 x 41
Finished size 1¼ x 1¼in (3.25 x 3.25cm)
Shown larger than actual size

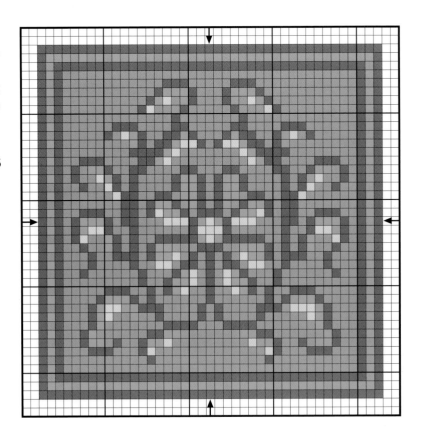

Georgian Cushion

	DMC	Anchor
	676	301
	781	309
	783	307
	931	977

William Morris Picture and Cushion

This tiny version of the Strawberry Thief is worked on fine 40 count silk gauze to create a delightful little picture, but you could add a border and a background and work the design on 32 count silk gauze to make a cushion.

The William Morris-inspired cushion is worked in Danish Flower threads, which have a matt finish and at this scale look more like tapestry wool than stranded cotton (floss) does, which is how this type of design would have originally appeared.

William Morris's career was wide ranging and extraordinarily successful. He was a poet, a writer, a scholar, an ardent socialist but above all a designer. He believed in the medieval ideal of craftsmanship – designer and workman should be one. He is well known for saying, 'Have nothing in your houses that isn't useful or you believe to be beautiful'. This adage applies just as well to a dolls' house.

The Strawberry Thief design was printed on chintz in about 1880 and has been reproduced on Liberty fabrics ever since in many different colourways. This miniature version is worked as a picture. The cushion would enhance a simple but stylish oak chair of the sort that Morris would have made.

Strawberry Thief Picture

You will need

2½ x 2½in (6 x 6cm) 40 count silk gauze

Size 28 tapestry needle

**DMC stranded cotton (floss) as follows
(Anchor conversions in brackets):**

dark red 355 (1014)

light red 356 (5975)

dark green 501 (878)

light green 503 (875)

dark blue 820 (134)

mid blue 322 (131)

light blue 3325 (128)

1 Fold the silk gauze in four to find the centre and mark it with a loose thread. Stitch the gauze into a fabric mount (see page 10).

2 Using one strand of stranded cotton (floss), work the design over one fabric thread from the chart below beginning at the centre and using continental tent stitch (see page 13). Take care not to run your thread behind any unworked areas where it will show through on the front.

3 Remove the finished picture from the fabric mount and refer to page 14 for pressing and framing.

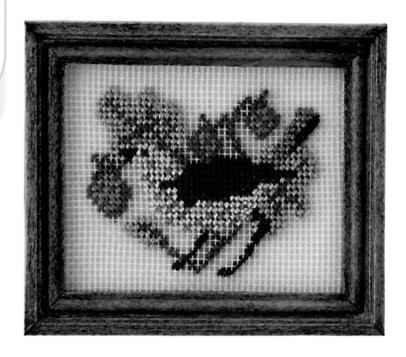

Stitch count 41 x 30
Finished size 1 x ¾in (2.6 x 1.9cm)
Shown larger than actual size

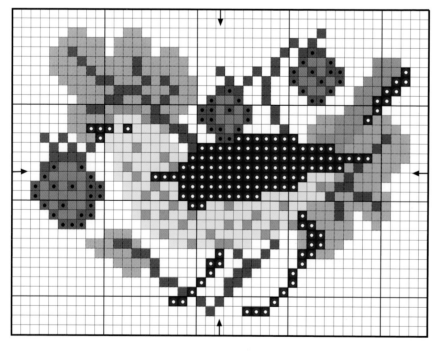

Strawberry Thief Picture

	DMC	Anchor
	322	131
	355	1014
	356	5975
	501	878
	503	875
	820	134
	3325	128

William Morris Cushion

You will need

3 x 3in (7.5 x 7.5cm) 32 count silk gauze

Size 28 tapestry needle

Danish Flower threads as follows:
dark blue/green 9; mid blue/green 224;
light blue/green 231; dark green 206;
light green 10; dark pink 96; mid pink 12;
light pink 113; dark gold 54;
light gold 46; blue background 220

1 Fold the silk gauze in four to find the centre, mark it with a loose thread and stitch the gauze into a fabric mount (see page 10).

2 Using one strand of Danish Flower thread, work the design over one fabric thread from the chart below, using continental tent stitch (see page 13) for the design and then diagonal tent stitch for the background.

3 Remove the embroidery from the fabric mount and press it carefully on the back (see page 14). Using one strand of blue, work a row of long-legged cross stitch (see page 12) around the edge of the square. Work in your hand and pull the stitches quite tightly and you will find that this stitch naturally folds the edge of the gauze and so makes a braided edge to your cushion. Now refer to page 15 for making up the cushion.

Stitch count 43 x 43
Finished size 1⅜ x 1⅜in (3.4 x 3.4cm)
Shown larger than actual size

William Morris Cushion

Danish Flower Thread

Symbol	Colour
▪	9
○	10
	12
	46
	54
	96
•	113
✕	206
	220
	224
	231

Victorian Bell Pull

This floral design is absolutely typical of Victorian Berlinwork. Substituting four shades of pink for four shades of gold and then adding a rich rust red background instead of cream changes the look completely, and there are many other variations that you could choose to go with your dolls' house décor. You will find a foot stool and two cushions or seat covers on pages 30–35 that all co-ordinate with this design. They all have pink or gold colourways and all will look equally good with cream or black backgrounds or even rust red for the gold variation.

You will need

2½ x 4½in (6.5 x 11.5cm) 32 count silk gauze

Size 28 tapestry needle

DMC stranded cotton (floss) as follows (Anchor conversions in brackets):

PINK COLOURWAY
dark pink 221 (43)
mid pink 223 (1023)
light pink 224 (1021)
very light pink 225 (1020)
purple 550 (101)
yellow 783 (307)
dark green 319 (218)
light green 320 (215)
dark sage green 3011 (844)
light sage green 3013 (842)
cream background 3033 (387)

GOLD COLOURWAY
dark gold 976 (1002)
mid gold 742 (306)
light gold 744 (305)
very light gold 746 (292)
purple 550 (101)
dark green 319 (218)
light green 320 (215)
dark sage green 3011 (844)
light sage green 3013 (842)
rust red background 3777 (341)

Two fine brass pins

In Victorian times every house belonging to the upper or middle classes would have a bell pull hanging in every room, usually by the fireplace. To call the maid you pulled the bell pull, a bell rang in the kitchen and your tea arrived as if by magic. Little brass dressmaker's pins make the rod at the top of this bell pull and a tiny tassel made from stranded cotton (floss) finishes the bottom and provides something to get hold of to summon the maid. Things are somewhat different these days and bell pulls have become purely decorative objects.

1 Fold the silk gauze in four to find the centre, mark it with a loose thread and stitch the gauze into a fabric mount (page 10).

2 Using two strands of stranded cotton (floss), work the design over one fabric thread from the chart, right, using continental tent stitch (see page 13) for the design and then diagonal tent stitch for the background.

3 Remove from the mount and press on the back (page 14). Using two strands of cream, work a row of long-legged cross stitch (page 12) around the edge. Work in your hand and pull the stitches quite tightly. You will find that this stitch naturally folds the edge of the gauze and so makes a braided edge to your bell pull.

Stitch count 17 x 85
Finished size ½ x 2⅝in (1.3 x 6.7cm)
Shown larger than actual size

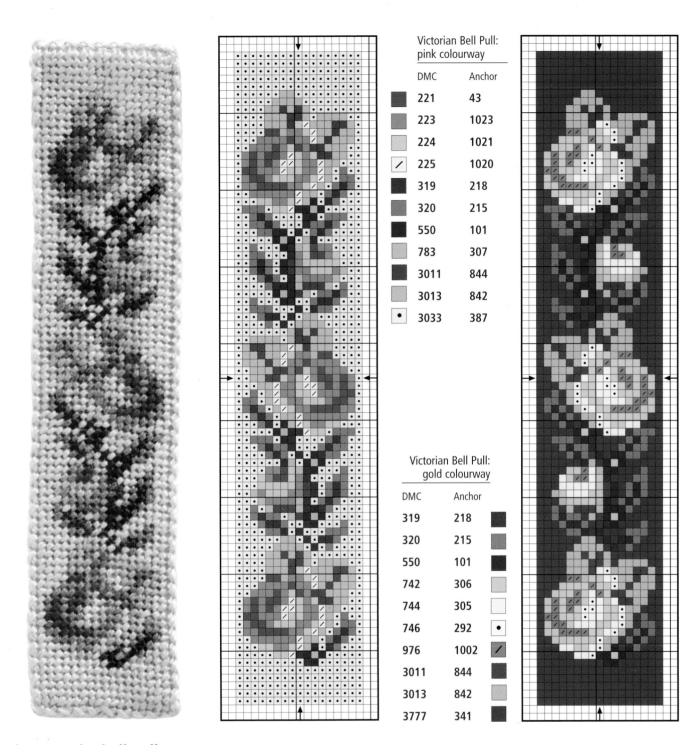

Victorian Bell Pull: pink colourway	
DMC	Anchor
221	43
223	1023
224	1021
225	1020
319	218
320	215
550	101
783	307
3011	844
3013	842
3033	387

Victorian Bell Pull: gold colourway	
DMC	Anchor
319	218
320	215
550	101
742	306
744	305
746	292
976	1002
3011	844
3013	842
3777	341

Making up the bell pull

1 Trim the silk gauze to ¼in (5mm) of the embroidery edge on the long sides. Fold the edges to the back and secure with herringbone stitch using ordinary sewing thread.

2 Make a tassel (page 14) in the same colour as your background and thread the cord through the bottom long-legged cross stitch edge, then trim this edge and herringbone it up.

3 The brass hanger is made from two wedding dress pins – special fine brass pins for silk, found at good haberdashery shops (notions departments). Lay two pins with a knob at both sides so that the knobs are the right distance apart for the width of the bell pull. Cut the ends off with a pair of wire cutters so the length of the pins overlap. Wrap a tiny piece of adhesive tape around them to hold them together. Trim the top edge of the gauze and

fold it to the back, tuck in the brass hanger and stitch the edge down with herringbone stitch.

4 Make a short length of twisted cord (see page 14) from two strands of stranded cotton (floss). Tie a knot in each end and trim the ends just below the knots to make little tassels on each end. Open up the twists of the cord and push the knobs of the hanger through on each side.

Blackwork Table Cover

Tablecloths are difficult to make for a dolls' house because the fabric is usually too thick to hang properly, so here is a way of solving the problem. Make a table top-sized cover rather than a draping cloth. The simple hem-stitched edge used is really useful too because there's no turning involved; the edge is stitched and then cut away, so you could make smaller mats just using fragments of this design. The stitching is actually a very dark brown which is just a little easier on the eye than black, though dark shades of red, green or blue are alternatives.

You will need

5 x 8in (12.5 x 20cm) 36 count ivory evenweave linen

Size 28 tapestry needle

DMC stranded cotton (floss) as follows (Anchor conversions in brackets):
dark brown 3371 (382)
cream ecru (2)

This table cover will suit a Tudor-style dolls' house. Blackwork was a popular decoration on dress as well as household linen especially during the medieval period and was used by the poorer classes to simulate expensive lacework.

So many examples of this type of stitchery appear in the works of the painter Hans Holbein (1497–1543) that one of the stitches has been named after him. True blackwork is worked in Holbein stitch, where running stitches are worked in one direction and then the alternate missing stitches are filled in on the journey back along the row, so you can hardly tell the back from the front. This table cover is worked in back stitch but do feel free to try Holbein stitch instead.

1 Fold the linen in four to find the centre and mark it with a loose thread. Work in your hand or in a frame if you prefer.

2 Using one strand of dark brown stranded cotton (floss) and back stitch (see page 11), work the main design over two fabric threads from the chart, beginning at the centre. Take care not to run your thread across any unstitched areas because the dark colour will show through on the front.

3 Using one strand of cream work simple hem stitch (see page 13) down each side of the cloth as shown on the chart. Take care to get this stitch the right way around (solid edge in, broken edge out), as it is the broken edge that can be cut up against. Pull your stitches tightly – this makes the edge neater and cutting easier because little holes open up to cut in and there are no loose threads to slip under the scissors.

4 Press well on the wrong side. Cut away the edges right up against the hem stitching. Cut the ends off ten threads beyond the end of the hem stitching and then fray out the ten threads to make a fringe. These frayed ends can then be sealed with a little Fray Check to prevent further threads coming loose later.

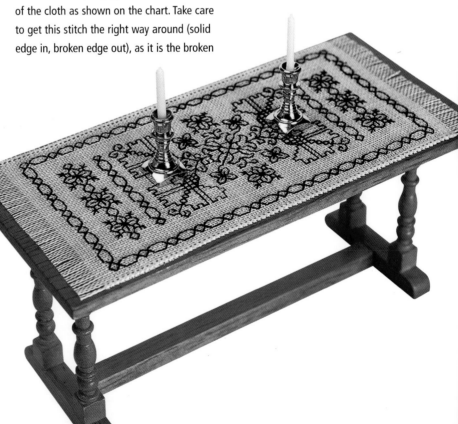

Stitch count 45 x 80
Finished size 2½ x 4½in (6.4 x 11.3cm)
Shown larger than actual size

Blackwork Table Cover

DMC	Anchor	
3371	382	(back stitch)
ecru	2	(hem stitch)

Victorian Foot Stool

The colour variations on this little foot stool co-ordinate with the bell pull on page 26 and the cushion and seat cover on page 32. The foot stool cleverly uses a covered button to make the pad so the embroidery is easy to mount but you could make a circular cushion instead. The circle would also sit perfectly on a miniature piano stool.

A foot stool makes a very decorative object in a Victorian room set. The full-size stools worked in Victorian times were often beaded as well as stitched but unfortunately it is not possible to miniaturize the glass beads sufficiently to accurately reflect dolls' house scale. Make sure that your dolls' house family put their slippers on before they put their feet on your fine embroidery.

You will need

3 x 3in (7.5 x 7.5cm) 32 count silk gauze

Size 28 tapestry needle

DMC stranded cotton (floss) as follows (Anchor conversions in brackets):

GOLD COLOURWAY
dark gold 976 (1002)
mid gold 742 (306)
light gold 744 (305)
very light gold 746 (292)
brown 839 (380)
dark green 936 (846)
mid green 3012 (843)
light green 3013 (842)
rust red background 3777 (341)

PINK COLOURWAY
dark pink 221 (43)
mid pink 223 (1023)
light pink 224 (1021)
very light pink 225 (1020)
yellow 783 (307)
dark green 936 (846)
mid green 3012 (843)
light green 3013 (842)
cream background 3033 (387)

Foot stool (see Suppliers page 62)

1 Fold the silk gauze in four to find the centre, mark it with a loose thread and stitch the gauze into a fabric mount (see page 10).

2 Using two strands of stranded cotton (floss), work the design over one fabric thread from the chart, right, using continental tent stitch (see page 13) for the design and then diagonal tent stitch for the background.

3 Remove the embroidery from the fabric mount and press it carefully on the back (see page 14). Refer to the manufacturer's instructions for fitting on to the foot stool.

Stitch count 34 x 34
Finished size 1¹⁄₁₆in (2.7cm) diameter
Shown larger than actual size

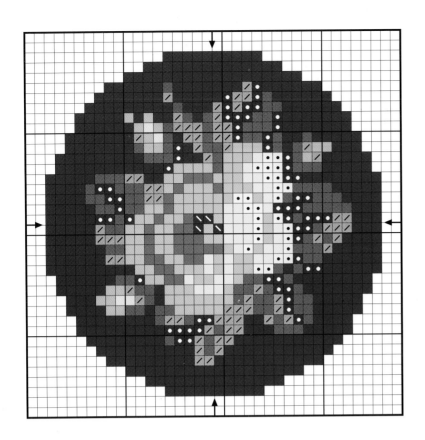

Foot Stool:
gold colourway

	DMC	Anchor
	742	306
	744	305
•	746	292
╲	839	380
⊙	936	846
	976	1002
	3012	843
╱	3013	842
	3777	341

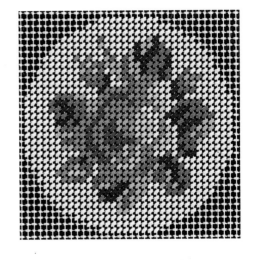

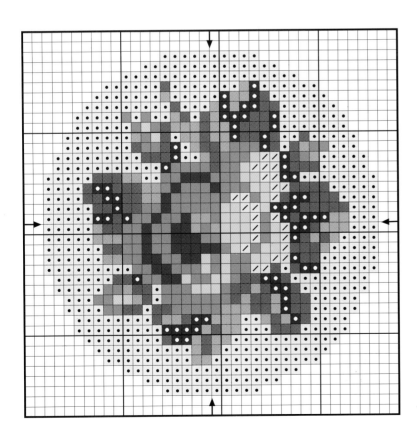

Foot Stool:
pink colourway

	DMC	Anchor
	221	43
	223	1023
	224	1021
╱	225	1020
	783	307
⊙	3033	387
	936	846
	3012	843
•	3013	842

Victorian Cushion and Seat Cover

These designs are really a pair of matching cushions but one has been stitched without the border and used to cover a chair seat. It is easy to remove the padded seat on a purchased chair and use the original cover as a pattern for the shape you wish to embroider. The padding and your embroidery can then be reassembled and glued back on to the chair.

The designs are worked on double canvas so they can be worked in petit point (small stitches) over one thread and the background filled in gros point, worked as cross stitch over the double threads. The floral motifs are worked in stranded cotton (floss) so the sheen stands out from the matt wool background. This method of stitching takes care but the effect is very authentic. If you prefer, you can work on 40 count silk gauze and use a single strand of stranded cotton (floss) throughout.

In the mid 19th century canvaswork became very popular, often worked in the same way as these cushions, with the design in fine petit point and the background in cross stitch. The designs were worked from hand-painted charts produced in Berlin in Germany and later in Britain. There were thousands of charts available, all very similar in style with animals, birds and flowers in abundance. The wools (yarns) used were dyed in Berlin and were very bright, however they were not very stable and quickly faded to much softer hues. The name 'Berlin woolwork' became synonymous with Victorian canvaswork.

You will need

3 x 3in (7.5 x 7.5cm) 20 count double canvas

Size 28 tapestry needle

DMC stranded cotton (floss) as follows (Anchor conversions in brackets):

PINK COLOURWAY
dark pink 221 (43); mid pink 223 (1023); light pink 224 (1021); very light pink 225 (1020); dark purple 550 (101); light purple 552 (99); yellow 783 (307); dark green 319 (218); light green 320 (215); dark sage green 3011 (844); light sage green 3013 (842); background DMC Medici wool noir

GOLD COLOURWAY
dark gold 976(1002); mid gold 742 (306); light gold 744 (305); very light gold 746 (292); dark purple 550 (101); light purple 552 (99); dark green 319 (218); light green 320 (215); dark sage green 3011 (844); light sage green 3013 (842); background DMC Medici wool rust red 8126

Victorian Cushion

1 Fold the canvas in four to find the centre, mark it with a loose thread and stitch the canvas into a fabric mount (see page 10).

2 Using two strands of stranded cotton (floss), work the complete design from the chart on page 33 (or one of the other designs and colourways on pages 34–35), using continental tent stitch (see page 13). To work over one thread you will need to prick out the canvas. Push your needle through the points where the threads are close together to separate them so the threads are no longer grouped in pairs but are evenly spaced. Just do this in the central area where the petit point will be.

3 Use a single strand of wool (yarn) for the background and work in cross stitch (see page 12) over double threads. Where you

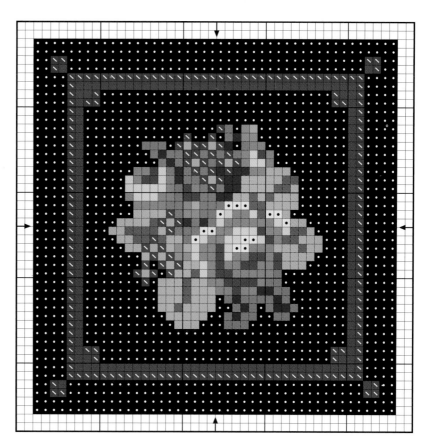

Victorian Cushion:
pink colourway

	DMC	Anchor
	221	43
	223	1023
	224	1021
●	225	1020
	319	218
	320	215
◥	550	101
	552	99
	783	307
	3011	844
	3013	842
●	DMC medici wool noir

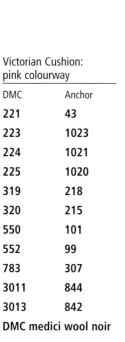

stitch up to the design there will be odd
single threads that you can fill with small tent
stitches as you work.

4 Remove the embroidery from the fabric
mount and press it carefully on the back
(see page 14). Using one strand of wool
(yarn), work a row of long-legged cross stitch
(see page 12) around the edge of the cushion
over a pair of canvas threads. Work in your
hand and pull the stitches quite tightly and
you will find that this stitch naturally folds the
edge of the canvas and so makes a braided
edge to your cushion. Refer to pages 14 and 15
for making up the cushion and adding tassels.

Stitch count 44 x 44
Finished size 1⅛ x 1⅛in (2.8 x 2.8cm)
Shown larger than actual size

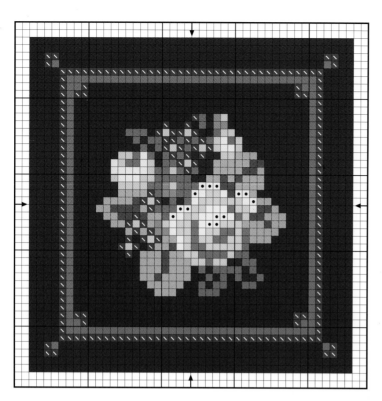

Victorian Cushion:
gold colourway

	DMC	Anchor		DMC	Anchor
■	319	218	•	746	292
■	320	215	■	976	1002
◪	550	101	■	3011	844
■	552	99	■	3013	842
■	742	306	■	DMC medici wool 8126	
□	744	305			

Victorian Seat Cover

You will need

3 x 3in (7.5 x 7.5cm) 20 count
double canvas

Size 28 tapestry needle

**DMC stranded cotton (floss) as follows
(Anchor conversions in brackets):**
PINK COLOURWAY
mid pink 223 (1023); light pink 224 (1021);
very light pink 225 (1020); dark green 936 (846);
mid sage green 3012 (844);
light sage green 3013 (842); light purple 552 (99);
dark purple 550 (101);
background DMC Medici wool noir

GOLD COLOURWAY
Mid gold 742 (306); light gold 744 (305);
very light gold 746 (292); dark green 936 (846);
mid sage green 3012 (844);
light sage green 3013 (842); light purple 552 (99);
dark purple 550 (101);
background DMC Medici wool rust red 8126

Clear multi-purpose glue

1 Either design can be stitched as a seat cover. Remove the original cover from the chair carefully and use this as a template. Take a piece of canvas and draw around your template, fold this to find the centre and work the design as described in the cushion instructions but omitting the border. Fill to the edges with the background colour.

2 Press carefully (see page 14) then trim away excess canvas and fold your embroidery over the original seat pad and glue back into place. Trim with a dolls' house braid if desired (see page 15 for instructions and page 62 for chair suppliers).

Stitch count 44 x 44
Finished size 1⅛ x 1⅛in (2.8 x 2.8cm)
Shown larger than actual size

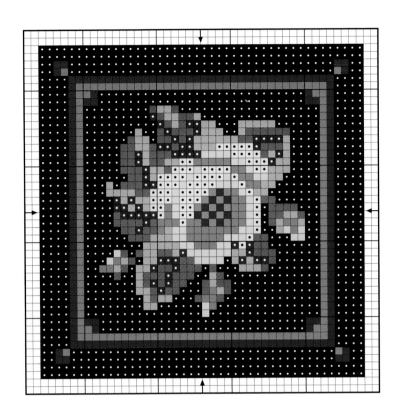

Victorian Seat Cover: pink colourway

	DMC	Anchor
	223	1023
	224	1021
•	225	1020
	550	101
	552	99
◉	936	846
	3012	844
	3013	842
◉	**Medici wool noir**	

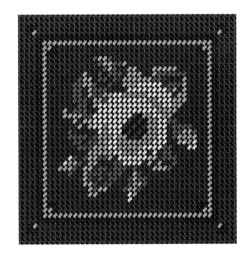

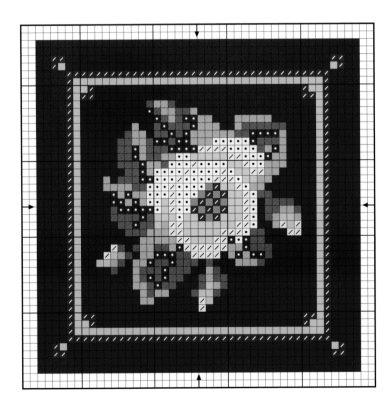

Victorian Seat Cover: gold colourway

	DMC	Anchor
╱	550	101
	552	99
	742	306
╱	744	305
•	746	292
◉	936	846
	3012	844
	3013	842
	DMC medici wool 8126	

Chinoiserie Bolster Cushion

This little bolster with its tassels just asks for an elegant *chaise-longue*. A day bed such as this can often be rather short on padding so a cushion is essential for the comfort of reclining ladies. There are two designs using the same colours so you could make one for each end of the chaise (see Suppliers page 62).

You will need

3 x 4in (7.5 x 10cm) 32 count silk gauze

Size 28 tapestry needle

DMC stranded cotton (floss) as follows (Anchor conversions in brackets):
dark blue 820 (134); mid blue 798 (146); light blue 794 (129); cream ecru (590); dark brown 3371 (382)

Cream silk dupion

A piece of felt or flannel

1 Fold the silk gauze in four to find the centre and mark it with a loose thread. Stitch the gauze into a fabric mount (see page 10).

2 Using two strands of stranded cotton (floss), work the design over one fabric thread from the chart, right, using continental tent stitch (see page 13) for the design and then diagonal tent stitch for the background.

3 Remove the embroidery from the fabric mount and press it carefully on the back (see page 14). Using two strands of dark blue, work a row of long-legged cross stitch (see page 12) along each long edge. Work in your hand and pull the stitches quite tightly and you will find that this stitch naturally folds the edge of the gauze and so makes a braided edge to your bolster.

Interest in anything Chinese suddenly had a great influence on interior design at the beginning of the 19th century. Rich merchants were travelling the world and bringing back textiles and china, and these things were avidly collected and displayed in the drawing rooms of the wealthy classes. The carp and dragon's head in these designs are traditional motifs and the blue and white colours are derived from Chinese porcelain.

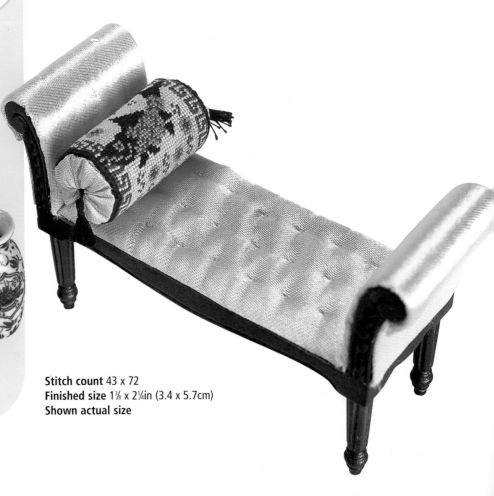

Stitch count 43 x 72
Finished size 1⅜ x 2¼in (3.4 x 5.7cm)
Shown actual size

36

Making up the bolster

1 First make two tassels in dark blue stranded cotton (floss) as described on page 14.

2 Trim the silk gauze to ⅜in (1cm) of the embroidery edge. Cut two strips of cream silk dupion the same length as the long sides of the embroidery and 1in (2.5cm) wide. Stitch these on to the long sides using a seam made on the wrong side as close as possible to the long-legged cross stitch edge. Put the two edges together to make the

seam along the length of the bolster and slipstitch it from the outside.

3 Make a roll of felt or flannel that is the same size as the embroidered part of the bolster and slide it inside. Stitch a row of running stitches around each end ⅜in (1cm) from the embroidery edge and trim the excess to ¼in (5mm). Pull up the running stitches to gather the end, tucking the ends in and the stalk of the tassel before you pull tight. Finish off the stitching.

Chinoiserie Bolster
Cushion: carp

	DMC	Anchor
	794	129
	798	146
	820	134
•	ecru	590

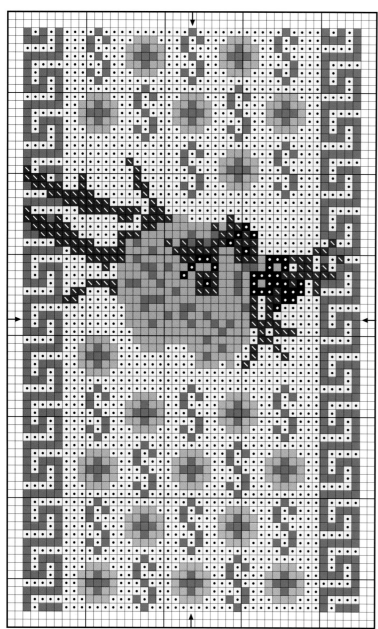

Chinoiserie Bolster Cushion: dragon's head

	DMC	Anchor
	794	129
	798	146
	820	134
	3371	382
•	ecru	590

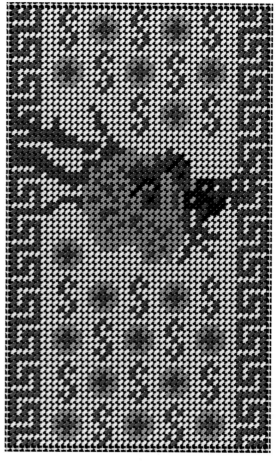

Art Nouveau Folding Screen

This room screen shows three different colourways stitched on the panels, so you can choose the one you prefer and work all the panels the same. The little screen was supplied as bare wood (see page 62) and has been painted with eggshell-finish emulsion paint – one of those little trial pots is ideal, they even have a brush in them. Once the panels are mounted add a finishing touch by drawing a gold line around each one with a gold felt-tip pen.

You will need

10 x 10in (25 x 25cm) (or enough to fill a small embroidery frame) sateen-finish curtain lining or glazed cotton (chintz)

Size 10 Straw or very fine Sharp needle

DMC stranded cotton (floss) as follows (Anchor conversions in brackets):

PINK/GREEN COLOURWAY
dark pink 223 (1023)
light pink 224 (1021)
dark green 3363 (266)
light green 524 (260)

BLUE COLOURWAY
dark blue 930 (1036)
mid blue 931 (1034)
light blue 932 (1033)

CREAM COLOURWAY
cream ecru (2)
pale gold 676 (300)

Tracing paper

Fine black felt-tip pen

Hard sharp pencil

Cream card

Polyester wadding (batting)

Clear all-purpose glue

Double-sided adhesive tape

Folding screen
(see Suppliers page 62)

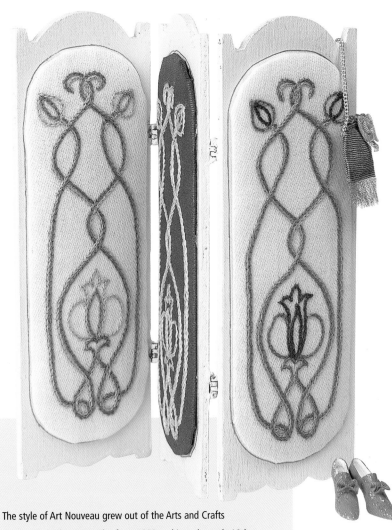

The style of Art Nouveau grew out of the Arts and Crafts movement and was popular from 1890 and into the early 19th century. It was inspired by flowing plant forms which were stylized and the designs appeared on many objects, including lamps, vases and furniture. The shapes are perfect for the panels of this little room screen which could be placed across a corner of an Art Nouveau dressing room.

Finished design size for each panel
1½ x 4¼in (3.8 x 10.8cm)
Shown smaller than actual size

Stitching and making up the screen

1 Trace the design template (see opposite page) on to tracing paper using a fine black felt-tip pen. Tape your tracing to a window pane and then tape the fabric over it. (Some photographic slide viewers work well for this or you can also use a blank but illuminated computer screen.) The outline will show through the fabric and you will be able to trace it using a hard sharp pencil. Draw three designs with at least 2in (5cm) between them.

2 Mount your fabric in an embroidery hoop or frame and use a single strand of stranded cotton (floss) throughout. Work the design in chain stitch (see page 11) referring to the pictures to place the colours. Once the stitching is complete, remove the fabric from the frame and press carefully on the wrong side (see page 14).

3 Trace the cutting and mounting templates provided (see opposite page). Cut three pieces of card using the mounting template and cut out the three embroidered panels using the cutting template. Take care to centre the embroideries in the panels.

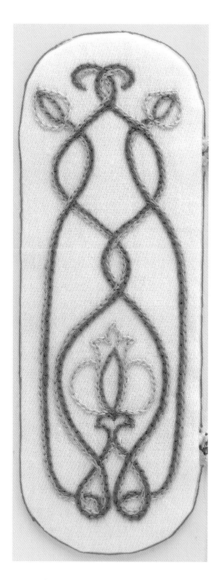

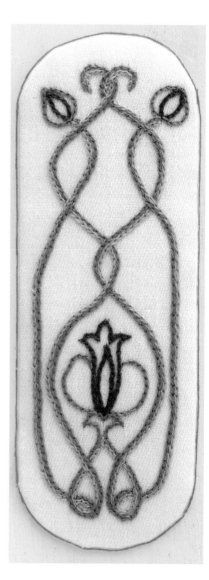

PINK/GREEN COLOURWAY CREAM COLOURWAY BLUE COLOURWAY

40

4 You only need a very thin layer of wadding (batting) for padding the panels; you should be able to pull polyester wadding apart in layers. Glue a thin layer to each piece of card and trim to the same size. Place the embroidery over the wadding and turn the edges over to the wrong side (clip the curves to do this) and hold them down with double-sided adhesive tape. Glue each embroidered panel top on one of the panels of the screen and weigh it down with a book while the glue dries. Outline the panels with a gold-tip pen if desired.

Design template

Fabric cutting template

Card mounting template

Clarice Cliff Fire Screen

This fire screen is actually just a picture frame with two little pieces of wood glued on to make feet. None of the fire screens available commercially were the right style for this Art Deco design which needed a simple shape. If your frame is a slightly different size just add or omit a few rows around the edges to make the design the right size.

You will need

3 x 4in (7.5 x 10cm) 32 count silk gauze

Size 28 tapestry needle

**DMC stranded cotton (floss) as follows
(Anchor conversions in brackets):**
dark orange 720 (326);
light orange 722 (323); yellow 742 (303);
mauve 3740 (872); black 310 (403);
cream ecru (590); blue 797 (139)

Fire screen (see Suppliers page 62)

1 Fold the silk gauze in four to find the centre, mark it with a loose thread and stitch the gauze into a fabric mount (see page 10).

2 Using two strands of stranded cotton (floss), work the design over one fabric thread from the chart, using continental tent stitch (see page 13) for the black lines, then diagonal tent stitch for the coloured areas.

3 Remove the embroidery from the fabric mount and press it carefully on the back. Refer to page 14 for stretching and then mount in the fire screen as for a sampler or according to the manufacturer's instructions.

Clarice Cliff was one of the best-known designers of ceramics from the Staffordshire Potteries in England in the 1930s. Her style was distinctive and unique; the shapes she favoured were angular and the colours extremely bright. Collectively the designs were known as Bizarre ware. The design used here is based on her Sunray design which was one of the most popular.

Stitch count 46 x 62
Finished size 1⁷⁄₁₆ x 1¹⁵⁄₁₆in (3.7 x 4.9cm)
Shown actual size

Clarice Cliff Fire Screen

	DMC	Anchor
■ (with dot)	310	403
■	720	326
▨	722	323
▨	742	303
■	797	139
■	3740	872
•	ecru	590

Florentine Seat Squab

This seat squab can be made any size to fit the seat or bench that you have. Begin your stitching with the dark green trail as shown on page 45 and simply keep going in either direction until your piece is the size required. This squab is worked in wool (yarn) on canvas to give a Tudor feel but you could change to stranded cotton (floss) on silk gauze for a finer, more sophisticated look. You could also change the colours to suit your dolls' house but choose sets of three shades of each colour and arrange them dark to light.

You will need

3 x 7in (7.5 x 18cm) 22 count canvas

Size 24 tapestry needle

Appletons crewel wool as follows:
dark green 336; mid green 334;
light green 332; dark blue 156;
mid blue 154; light blue 152;
dark gold 695; mid gold 694;
light gold 692; mauve 933

1 You can work this design in your hand or mount the canvas into a frame if you prefer. If you work in your hand take care not to pull the long stitches too tight. Use one strand of crewel wool throughout. Begin working with the dark green (336) row (charted separately opposite to get you going), then work the mid green row below it. All the stitches are vertical lines worked over two or four threads.

2 Continue through the colour sequence in either direction, then fill in the triangular shapes at the top with mauve tent stitch (see page 13) and the bottom with light gold. Remove the work from the frame if you have been using one.

3 Using one strand of mauve work a row of long-legged cross stitch (see page 12) around the edge. Work in your hand and pull the stitches quite tightly and you will find that this stitch naturally folds the edge of the canvas and so makes a braided edge to your seat squab.

4 Trim the edges of the canvas to about ⅜in (1cm), fold them back and stitch them down on to the back of the work with herringbone stitch (see page 12) using ordinary sewing thread. You can leave the back like this or line it with a scrap of silk in a suitable colour just turned in and slipstitched on.

Florentine or Bargello work was extremely popular in the late 17th century, the names probably deriving from the Bargello Palace in Florence, Italy. These patterns are lovely for upholstery or furniture covers because the repeating patterns can simply be worked over and over again until the right size and shape is reached. The canvas is covered quite quickly and the resulting fabric is fairly hardwearing. This particular pattern is called Gothic Pinnacles and it would look splendid on an oak settle in a Tudor hallway.

Stitch count 19 x 99
Finished size ⅞ x 4½in (2.2 x 11.4cm)
Shown larger than actual size

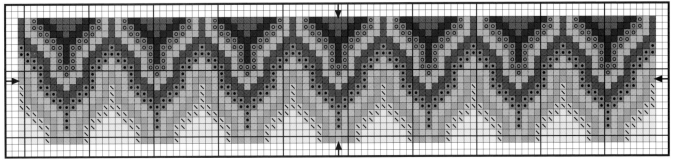

Florentine Seat Squab

Appletons crewel wool

▨	152	▨	336
◉	154	▨	692
▨	156	╲	694
▨	332	▨	695
•	334	▨	933

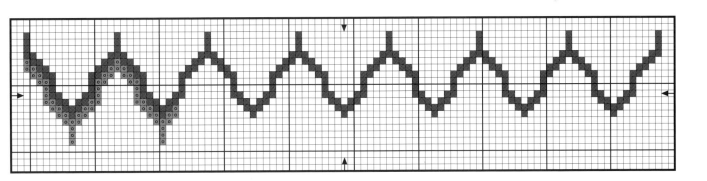

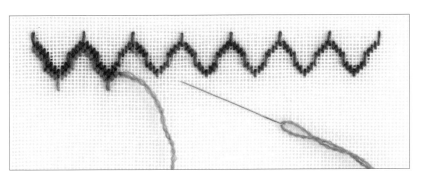

Follow this part-chart to begin, as described in step 1, working the dark green row (336) in long stitch. Change to mid green (334) and work along that row, and so on.

Georgian Pole Screen

This little bird picture is stitched on fine 40 count silk gauze because the frame is so small that unless the stitching is very fine it is not possible to get enough detail into the picture. If your eyes really will not cope with such a high count then use a lower one and just stitch the bird on its branch and fill the background to size in cream with a straight green border perhaps.

You will need

3 x 3in (7.5 x 7.5cm) 40 count
silk gauze

Size 28 tapestry needle

**DMC stranded cotton (floss) as follows
(Anchor conversions in brackets):**
dark coral 356 (338)
dark blue 806 (162);
light blue 3766 (1039);
dark green 501 (878);
light green 503 (875);
brown 839 (380);
yellow 783 (307);
light coral 352 (337);
cream 677 (386)

Pole screen (see Suppliers page 62)

1 Fold the silk gauze in four to find the centre, mark it with a loose thread and stitch the gauze into a fabric mount (see page 10).

2 Using one strand of stranded cotton (floss), work the design over one fabric thread from the chart, using continental tent stitch (see page 13) for the design and then diagonal tent stitch for the backgrounds.

3 Remove the embroidery from the fabric mount and press it carefully on the back (see page 14). Remove the frame from your pole screen and mount the embroidery according to the manufacturer's instructions.

A Georgian pole screen had a very practical purpose as well as being a very decorative object. The lady would sit by the roaring fire (the only heat source so she would want to get close) and to avoid a red face she would position the pole screen so that her face was screened from the heat. Now that we have central heating in our homes these pretty things have become collector's items. Not many have survived as they are quite delicate even at full size; the miniature versions are even more delicate and pretty. Place this one by the fireplace in a Georgian sitting room.

Stitch count 51 x 51
Finished size 1¼ x 1¼in (3.2 x 3.2cm)
Shown larger than actual size

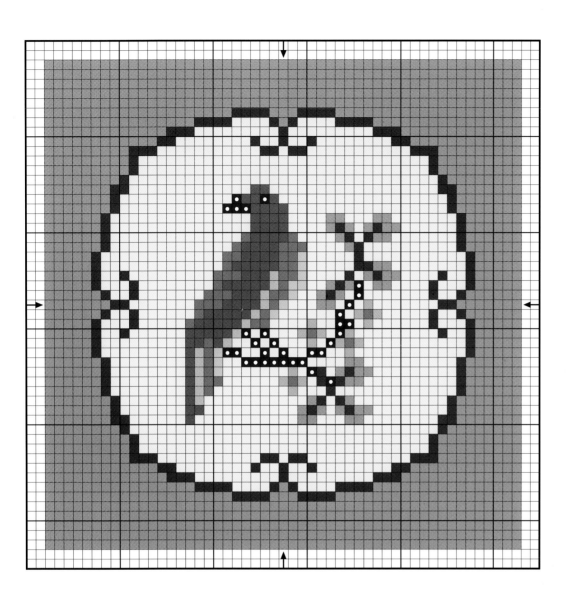

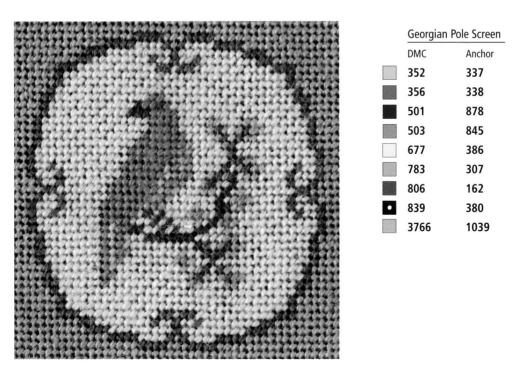

Georgian Pole Screen

	DMC	Anchor
	352	337
	356	338
	501	878
	503	845
	677	386
	783	307
	806	162
	839	380
	3766	1039

Regency Cushion

This classical design is shown in two different colourways but you could change them to match your other dolls' house furnishings. The cushion is shown here partly worked on a miniature embroidery frame, just as though the lady of the house has left her embroidery to go on a visit but is intending to be back soon to resume her stitching.

You will need

3 x 3in (7.5 x 7.5cm) 32 count silk gauze

Size 28 tapestry needle

DMC stranded cotton (floss) as follows (Anchor conversions in brackets):

PINK COLOURWAY
dark pink 3721 (896)
mid pink 223 (895)
light pink 224 (893)
very light pink 225 (892)
dark blue/green 502 (876)
light blue/green 504 (1042)
dark green 3051 (268)
light green 3053 (265)

GOLD COLOURWAY
dark yellow 783 (306)
mid yellow 676 (295)
light yellow 677 (292)
cream ecru (590)
dark blue 931 (1034)
light blue 3752 (1032)
dark green 3051 (268)
light green 3053 (265)

1 Fold the silk gauze in four to find the centre, mark it with a loose thread and stitch the gauze into a fabric mount (see page 10).

2 Using two strands of stranded cotton (floss), work the design over one fabric thread from the chart, using continental tent stitch (see page 13) for the design and then diagonal tent stitch for the background and wide stripes. If you are going to mount the embroidery on a frame, as shown in the picture, stop before the embroidery is finished. To make up into a cushion, carry on and finish the embroidery.

3 Remove the embroidery from the fabric mount and press it carefully on the back (see page 14). To mount on a frame, trim the sides of gauze to the width of the frame and put a little Fray Check on them to prevent the gauze from fraying. Fold the top and bottom over the rollers of the frame and stitch in place with little running stitches and then trim away the excess.

4 To make a cushion, use two strands of mid pink to work a row of long-legged cross stitch (see page 12) around the edge of the square. Work in your hand and pull the stitches quite tightly and you will find that this stitch naturally folds the edge of the gauze and so makes a braided edge to your cushion. Refer to page 15 for making up the cushion.

During the Regency period nearly everything was covered either in flowers or stripes or even better, both at once. The decorative palette had suddenly become much brighter and varied and luxury textiles were being imported from all over the world. All the large cities of Europe prospered and the houses in them reflected this prosperity.

Stitch count 37 x 37
Finished size 1⅛ x 1⅛in (2.9 x 2.9cm)
Shown slightly larger than actual size

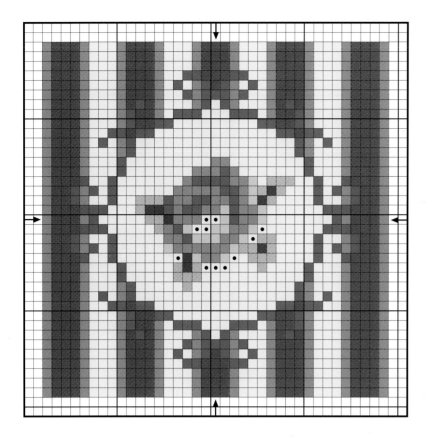

Regency Cushion:
pink colourway

	DMC	Anchor
	223	895
	224	893
•	225	892
	502	876
	504	1042
	3051	268
	3053	265
	3721	896

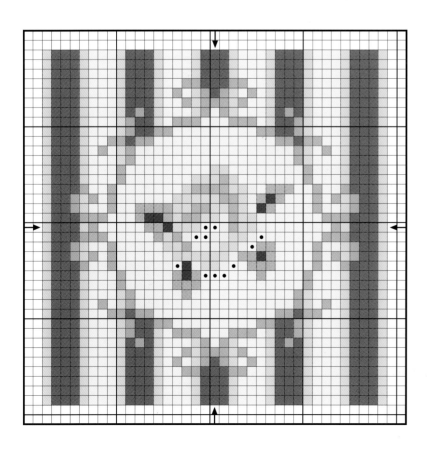

Regency Cushion:
gold colourway

	DMC	Anchor
	676	295
	677	292
	783	306
	931	1034
	3051	268
	3053	265
	3752	1032
•	ecru	590

49

Regency Fire Screen

This little fire screen is worked using nearly the same silk threads as the Georgian chair seat on page 20 so they will look lovely together in the same room. It is created using very fine free embroidery in pure silk – do try it because you will be surprised how easy it is and the result is so charming. The fabric is sateen curtain lining but you could use any closely woven natural fabric.

A bird sitting amongst fruits and flowers is the traditional picture for a fire screen and this one is very exotic with his pink and purple feathers. Strawberries are the most English of fruits and appear in embroideries from medieval times to the present day.

**Finished size 1½ x 2in (4 x 5cm)
Shown actual size**

You will need

3 x 3in (7.5 x 7.5cm) (or enough to fill a small embroidery frame) sateen-finish cream curtain lining

Size 10 Straw or any very fine Sharp needle

Caron Soie Cristale silk thread as follows:
purple 6021; red 2013; pink 2032; cream 4007; yellow 4003; dark green 5002; light green 5004; brown 3061

Single strand of dark brown stranded cotton (floss)

Tracing paper

Fine black felt-tip pen

Hard sharp pencil

Fire screen (see Suppliers page 62)

1 First trace the design outline provided below on to tracing paper using a fine black felt-tip pen. Tape your tracing to a window pane and then tape the fabric over it. (Some photographic slide viewers work well for this or you can also use a blank but illuminated computer screen.) The outline will show through the fabric and you will be able to trace it using a hard sharp pencil.

2 Mount your fabric in an embroidery hoop or frame and use a single strand of the silk throughout. See pages 11–13 for working all the stitches. Using dark green, outline the leaves in split back stitch – this creates a raised effect on the edges of the leaves and also makes it much easier to make a straight edge to the satin/straight stitches when they are stitched over the split back stitch. Now work straight stitches from the edge of the leaf to the central vein: take care with the direction of these stitches as they need to be in the direction that the small veins on the leaves would be. They will be closer together at the central vein than at the leaf edge so that they fan out around the point.

3 Cover the area of each strawberry with red long and short stitch; your stitches should radiate out at the top of the fruit and in again at the bottom. Work each row into the stitches of the last layer. The little light green leaves at the top of each fruit are just straight stitches that radiate out from the bottom of each little leaf to fill it. Scatter tiny stitches in yellow over the surface of each strawberry.

6 Work the hills at the bottom in chain stitch. Work the first top row in dark green on the line and then below it work a row of light green close to it and then a row of yellow below that.

7 Work the body of the bird and the tail in pink long and short stitch. Begin at the top of the head and work down the body shaping it with your stitches. Now work the wing in purple and then add a few random stitches in purple to the chest and tail. The feet are just two or three stitches in dark brown stranded cotton (floss) and the legs a single straight stitch. The beak is yellow with a straight stitch in dark brown over it. Finally, add a French knot for an eye in dark brown.

8 Press the embroidery carefully on the back (see page 14). Mount the embroidery in your fire screen according to the manufacturer's instructions.

4 Now work the little flowers, radiating straight stitches in cream out from the centre of each flower. Use dark green to work a straight stitch between each petal and then a yellow French knot in the centre.

5 Use stem stitch to work all the stems in brown. Take care where the stems divide: work the main one and then join in again very close to the first line of stitching and a little way back from the divide, so there is no gap and the stems look as though they grew rather than were stuck together.

51

Tudor Rose Floor Cushion

This Tudor rose design is stitched in tent stitch with a line of split back stitch added to create a three-dimensional effect to the petals. This smoothes out the edges of the design and makes the flower stand out from the background. Traditionally the Tudor rose is in shades of pink but there are charts of blue and mauve alternatives on page 55 so that you can match your colour schemes or make a set if you like.

You will need

3 x 3in (7.5 x 7.5cm) 32 count silk gauze

Size 28 tapestry needle

DMC stranded cotton (floss) as follows (Anchor conversions in brackets):

PINK COLOURWAY
dark pink 223 (1023)
mid pink 224 (1021)
light pink 225 (1020)
green 3347 (226)
yellow 783 (307)
dark green background 500 (683)
dark pink outline 315 (972)

BLUE COLOURWAY
dark blue 930 (1035)
mid blue 931 (1034)
light blue 3752 (1033)
green 3011 (844)
yellow 676 (301)
cream background ecru (590)
dark blue outline 3750 (150)

MAUVE COLOURWAY
dark mauve 3740 (873)
mid mauve 3041 (872)
light mauve 3042 (870)
green 520 (861)
pink 778 (969)
light green background 524 (858)
claret outline 902 (972)

Backing fabric

Polyester filling

This is quite a big cushion and so can be used on the floor rather than in a chair. Here it is made with a boxed bottom piece and corner tassels. If you want to make it smaller work either on 40 count silk gauze or omit the border.

Stitch count 55 x 55
Finished size 1¾ x 1¾in (4.4 x 4.4cm)
Shown larger than actual size

1 Fold the silk gauze in four to find the centre, mark it with a loose thread and stitch the gauze into a fabric mount (see page 10).

2 Using two strands of stranded cotton (floss), work the design over one fabric thread from the chart, right, using continental tent stitch (see page 13) for the design and then diagonal tent stitch for the background. Using one strand of dark pink (if stitching the pink colourway), work split back stitch (see page 13) around the petal edges, the turned-in edges and the central circle.

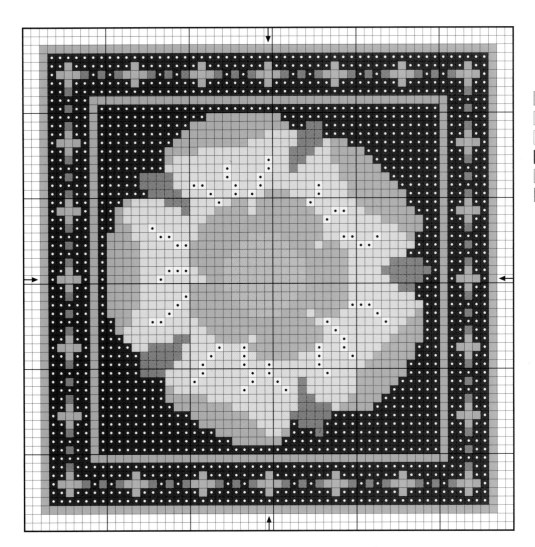

Tudor Rose Cushion:
pink colourway

DMC	Anchor
223	1023
224	1021
225	1020
500	683
783	307
3347	226

3 Remove the embroidery from the fabric mount and press it carefully on the back (see page 14). Using two strands of dark pink work a row of long-legged cross stitch (see page 12) around the edge of the square. Work in your hand and pull the stitches quite tightly and you will find that this stitch naturally folds the edge of the gauze and so makes a braided edge to your cushion. See the next page for making up your cushion.

Making up the boxed-floor cushion

1 First make four tassels using mixed stranded cotton (floss) colours, as described on page 14.

2 Trim the silk gauze to ⅜in (1cm) of the embroidery edge and then cut a piece of backing fabric 1in (2.5cm) bigger on each side.

3 Draw a square in the centre of the backing fabric the same size as the embroidered area using a pencil or tailor's chalk (see diagram). Fold one corner diagonally and sew from the point of the square to the edge of the fabric to make a box shape. Repeat for the other corners.

4 Turn in the edges of the box and slipstitch the embroidered top on, tucking a tassel into each corner and leaving a gap in the last side. Fill the cushion firmly before you complete the slipstitching. You will find that the tassels stick out on stalks so just catch them down to the side seams of the cushion.

	fold	seam line		seam line	fold	
seam line						seam line
			Square the same size as the embroidered area			
seam line						seam line
	fold	seam line		seam line	fold	

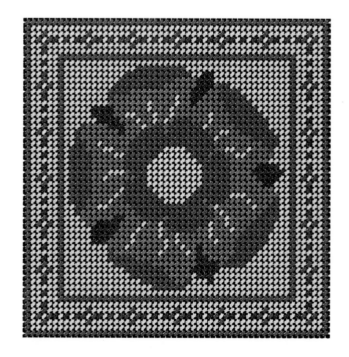

Tudor Rose Cushion:
blue colourway

	DMC	Anchor
	676	301
	930	1035
	931	1034
	3011	844
/	3752	1033
•	ecru	590

Tudor Rose Cushion:
mauve colourway

	DMC	Anchor
	520	861
	524	858
	778	969
	3041	872
•	3042	870
	3740	873

55

Edwardian Bed Linen

This embroidered bed linen was made from a fine cotton handkerchief and the lovely hem-stitched edge was already there. One lady's handkerchief (the kind that used to come folded in birthday cards from Great Aunts) will make the sheet and bolster but if you want to make an under sheet as well you will need two. The blanket is made from a piece of old-fashioned flannel with the edge worked in pink blanket stitch. The flannel was cut to just the right size so that the edge shows rather than tucking it in. The bolster is made from a roll of the same flannel but if you can't find flannel a piece of cream felt will be fine.

You will need

Fine cotton lawn or a handkerchief with a hem-stitched edge for the sheet

A piece of flannel for the bolster

Size 10 Straw or any very fine Sharp needle

DMC stranded cotton (floss) as follows (Anchor conversions in brackets):
blue 932 (977)
pink 223 (1023)
yellow 676 (301)
mauve 3041 (872)
green 3012 (843)

Tracing paper

Fine black felt-tip pen

Hard sharp pencil

Fabrics that drape are difficult to work in the dolls' house because at this size the fabric sticks out rather than hangs down as it would at full size, so this bed does not have a cover but shows the embroidered linen that can be tucked in. You could place a folded cover on the end of the bed.

To make the sheet

1 Decide where the design is to go on your handkerchief by folding it and placing it on the bed and cutting the fabric the right size to make a sheet with a wide turnover.

2 Trace the black outline provided, right, on to tracing paper using a fine black felt-tip pen. Tape your tracing of the outline to a window pane and then tape the handkerchief over it so that the design is in the right place. (Some photographic slide viewers work well for this or you can also use a blank but illuminated computer screen). The outline will show through the fabric and you will be able to trace it using a hard sharp pencil.

**Finished design size 1½ x 1in (4 x 2.5cm)
Shown smaller than actual size**

56

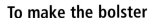

3 Mount in an embroidery hoop or frame and use a single strand of stranded cotton (floss) throughout. See pages 11–13 for working all the stitches. Use green to work the leaves, making satin/straight stitches from the edge of the leaf to the central vein. Take care with the direction of these stitches – they need to be in the direction that the small veins on the leaves would be, closer together at the central vein than at the leaf edge so they fan out around the point. Work all the stems in green stem stitch.

To make the bolster

1 Roll up a piece of flannel that is just a bit narrower than your bed until it makes a roll of the right size. Cut a piece of fine cotton fabric to cover this roll with enough for a seam along the length and spare at the ends for gathering up.

2 Turn your tracing over and trace a mirror image of the design on to the fabric so that it is in the right place on the bolster. Work the embroidery as for the sheet.

3 Wrap the embroidered cover around the bolster roll and slipstitch the seam from the outside, making sure that the embroidery sits in the right place. Stitch a row of running stitches around each end and pull these up to gather the end, tucking the ends inside the gather. Finish off the stitching.

4 Work the little flowers in pink detached chain stitch and fill the centres with a cluster of yellow French knots. Add a cluster of mauve French knots to the ends of the three stalks. Work the bow with its trailing ends in blue chain stitch.

5 Now either hem stitch the edges of the sheet or simply seal them with Fray Check as they are not going to show. Cover the mattress with another piece of handkerchief as a bottom sheet.

Georgian House Sampler

This charming little sampler is worked on fine 40 count silk gauze, using one strand of stranded cotton (floss). If this is too fine for you just work the house on 32 count or stitch the whole design and buy a bigger frame. You could omit the whitework panel and substitute your initials to personalize the sampler. Do take care not to run any threads across the back of your work because they will show through the gauze where it is not covered with stitching.

You will need

2½ x 2½in (6 x 6cm)
40 count silk gauze

Size 28 tapestry needle

DMC stranded cotton (floss) as follows
(Anchor conversions in brackets):
dark red 355 (1014)
light red 356 (1013)
yellow 783 (307)
brown 801 (358);
green 936 (846)
blue 930 (1035)
light grey 414 (235)
dark grey 413 (236)
cream ecru (590)

This sampler is typical of many made in the 18th century. The red brick house, the trees and spot motifs of birds, flowers and a crown can be found over and over again on full-sized samplers from this period. This one also has a whitework panel at the bottom: at full size this would have been a piece of cut work; as a miniature it can only be worked in tent stitch and back stitch.

1 Fold the silk gauze in four to find the centre, mark it with a loose thread and stitch the gauze into a fabric mount (see page 10).

2 Using one strand of stranded cotton (floss), work the design over one fabric thread from the chart, using continental tent stitch (see page 13). Begin with the house, from the centre, and then count out from there to the other motifs. Once you have worked the two intertwining hearts in ecru tent stitch work the border to them in ecru back stitch (see page 11)

3 Remove the finished sampler from the fabric mount and refer to page 14 for pressing and framing.

Stitch count 36 x 44
Finished size ¹⁵⁄₁₆ x 1⅛in (2.3 x 2.8cm)
Shown actual size

Georgian House Sampler

DMC	Anchor	
355	1014	
356	1013	
413	236	
414	235	
783	307	
801	358	
930	1035	
936	846	
ecru	590	
ecru	590	back stitch

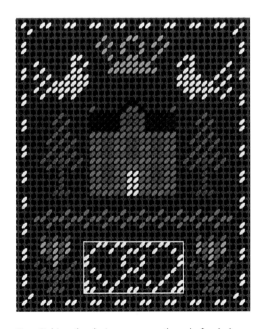

Try stitching the design over one thread of a dark blue or purple 32 count linen for a dramatic effect, changing the dark blue 930 (1035) colour to ecru.

Mackintosh Chair Cover

The chair is a copy of one designed by Charles Rennie Mackintosh (see page 62 for suppliers). The one shown here is made of dark wood and the darker of the two colour variations looks well on it. If your chair is in lighter wood you could use the lighter-coloured variation or re-colour the design to fit into your dolls' house. The chair has quite a small seat but if you have a larger one just extend the design to fit.

You will need

3 x 3in (7.5 x 7.5cm) 32 count silk gauze

Size 28 tapestry needle

DMC stranded cotton (floss) as follows (Anchor conversions in brackets):

PINK COLOURWAY
dark pink 3687 (1027);
mid pink 3688 (895)
light pink 3713 (893)
jade 502 (875)
dark brown 3031 (1050)

PURPLE COLOURWAY
dark purple 552 (101)
mid purple 553 (99)
light purple 554 (97)
cream ecru (590)
dark brown 3371 (382)

Mackintosh chair (see Suppliers page 62)

Charles Rennie Mackintosh (1868–1928) was a famous Art Nouveau designer and architect from Glasgow in Scotland. He worked with his wife, Margaret Macdonald Mackintosh, who was an artist and whose influence on him was enormous. There are still numerous examples of his work in Glasgow where he designed whole buildings complete with their interiors and furnishings. The Rennie Mackintosh pink rose is one of his most famous designs, often reproduced since his death and here is a dolls' house version. This little chair would be dated about 1900 and will be perfect for an Art Nouveau room set.

Stitch count 42 x 36
Finished size 1⁵⁄₁₆ x 1⅛in (3.3 x 2.9cm)
Shown actual size

1 Fold the silk gauze in four to find the centre, mark it with a loose thread and stitch the gauze into a fabric mount (see page 10).

2 Using two strands of stranded cotton (floss), work the design over one fabric thread from the chart, using continental tent stitch (see page 13) for the dark brown design lines and then diagonal tent stitch to fill in the shapes and the background.

3 Remove the embroidery from the fabric mount and press it carefully on the back (see page 14). Cover the seat pad and fix it to your chair following the instructions given on page 15.

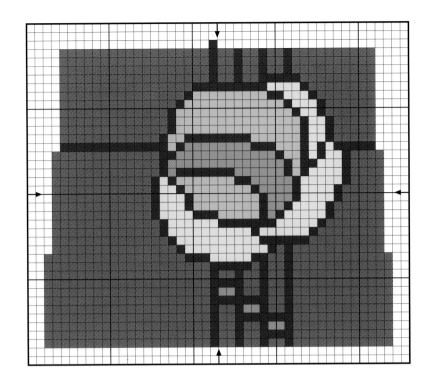

**Mackintosh Chair Cover:
pink colourway**

	DMC	Anchor
	502	3013
	1050	875
	3687	1027
	3688	895
	3713	893

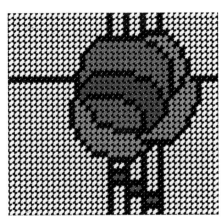

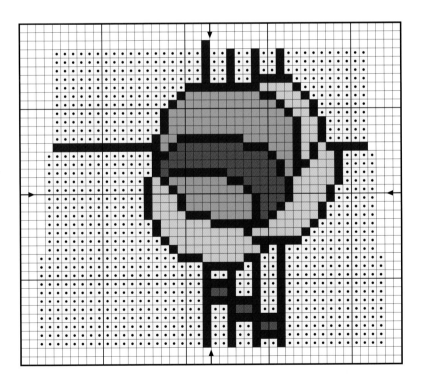

**Mackintosh Chair Cover:
purple colourway**

	DMC	Anchor
	552	101
	553	99
	554	97
	3371	382
•	ecru	590

61

Suppliers

Appletons Bros Ltd
Thames Works, Church Street,
Chiswick, London WE 2PE, UK
tel: 0181 994 0711
For tapestry wools

Burford Needlecraft Centre
117 High Street, Burford, Oxon.
OX18 4RG, UK
tel: 01993 822136
www.needlework.co.uk
Mail order for threads and fabrics

Caron Threads
Macleod Craft Marketing, West
Yonderton, Warlock Road, Bridge of
Weir, Renfrewshire, PA11 3SR,
Scotland
tel: 01505 612618
For Caron threads

Coats Crafts UK
PO Box 22, Lingfield Estate,
McMullen Road, Darlington,
County Durham, DL1 1YQ, UK
tel: 01325 365457 (for stockists)
*For a wide range of needlework
supplies, including Anchor threads*

DMC Creative World Ltd
Pullman Road, Wigston,
Leicestershire LE18 2DY, UK
tel: 0116 281 1040 (for stockists)
fax: 0116 281 3592
www.dmc/cw.com
*For a full range of needlework supplies,
including threads and Zweigart fabrics*

The Dolls' House Draper
PO Box 128, Lightcliffe, Halifax,
West Yorkshire HX3 8RN
Tel: 01422 201275
Dolls' house fabrics and trimmings

Dolls House Emporium
Write or telephone for free colour
catalogue, quoting EDC1: EDC1,
Ripley, Derbyshire, DE5 3YD, UK
tel: 01773 514400
www.dollshouse.com
For a wide range of dolls' house supplies

Ivydene Miniatures
28 Sixth Avenue, Chelmsford,
Essex CM1 4ED
tel: 01245 495851
For furniture and silk gauze

Jojays
Moore Road, Bourton-on-the-
Water, Glous GL54 2AZ, UK
tel: 01451 810081
www.jojays.co.uk
www.jojays.com
*Dolls' houses and miniatures specialist
shop stocking just about everything for
the dolls' house*

Needleworks by Sue Hawkins
East Wing, Highfield House, School
Lane, Whitminster, Gloucestershire
GL2 7PJ, UK
*Sue Hawkins' company supplies
counted canvaswork, crewelwork and
cross stitch kits as well as upholstered
embroidery frames. For a catalogue
write (enclosing five 1st class stamps)
or telephone 01452 740118*

The Silk Route
Cross Cottage, Cross Lane, Frimley
Green, Surrey GU16 6LN
Tel: 01252 835781
Silk in small quantities

The Viking Loom
22 High Petergate, York, North
Yorkshire YO1 2EH, UK
tel: 01904 620587
www.vikingloom.co.uk
Mail order for threads and fabrics

SUPPLIERS OF FURNITURE USED
THROUGHOUT THE BOOK (SEE
ABOVE FOR CONTACT DETAILS):
The Dolls House Emporium:
table page 28; chair page 32; chaise
page 36; bed page 56; chair page 60.
Ivydene Miniatures:
picture frames pages 17, 23 & 58;
chair page 20; foot stool page 30; pole
screen page 46; fire screen page 50.
Jojays:
Folding three-part frame page 39;
fire screen page 42; bench page 44;
embroidery frame page 48.

Acknowledgments

My thanks to Cheryl Brown at David and Charles for commissioning this book the day we moved house and still trusting me to do it on time (which I did); to Steve and Cherry for giving me a wonderful, spacious, comfortable roof over my head while I worked; to Lin Clements for such diligent editing; to Jane Greenoff for all the old flannel (it was to make the blanket but I simply could not resist putting that in print); to Pauline Cooper for the beautiful soft kapok to fill the tiny cushions that she gathered from the trees in Madeira and brought to me so prettily packaged; to the lady at Ivydene Miniatures who persuaded her husband to make and polish the furniture she supplied; to Zweigart for supplies of fine canvas; to Macleod Craft Marketing for their generosity with their lovely threads from the Caron Collection; to John, Hannah and Jo for putting up with me and last, but definitely not least, to my two spaniels Billy and Tommy, who keep me company while I work, take me out for walks and make me laugh.

About the Author

Sue Hawkins began her career working for an antique dealer, restoring seventeenth-century English embroidery. Her knowledge of the needlework business was gained whilst owning and running an embroidery shop for several years, and since 1991 she has designed for and run her own successful kit-manufacturing company, Needleworks (see Suppliers). Sue also teaches embroidery workshops at her home and around the country. Many of the workshops are run on behalf of the Cross Stitch Guild, of which she is technical director. This is Sue's fifth book for David & Charles, her last one being *Dolls House DIY: Carpets and Rugs*. Sue lives near Stroud, Gloucestershire, UK.

Index